Indian Nations
of Wisconsin

Indian Nations of Wisconsin

Histories of Endurance and Renewal

Patty Loew

WISCONSIN HISTORICAL SOCIETY PRESS

Madison

Published by the
WISCONSIN HISTORICAL SOCIETY PRESS

Printed in the United States of America
Designed by Jane Tenenbaum
Maps produced by Amelia Janes and Mike Gallagher, Midwest Educational Graphics

Cover photos: Center photo by A. C. Stone, WHi(X3)32712; upper right photo courtesy of *Potawatomi Traveling Times*; bottom left and bottom right photos courtesy of Lac Courte Oreilles Band of Lake Superior Chippewa; bottom center photo courtesy of Frank Montano.
Illustration on page iii: Ojibwe spearfishing in winter. (Sketch by Seth Eastman; WHi(X3)13551)
Photo on page v: Courtesy of Patty Loew. Photos on page vii: left, courtesy of Oneida Nation; center, courtesy of Lac Courte Oreilles Band of Lake Superior Chippewa; right, courtesy of St. Croix Band of Lake Superior Chippewa.

05 04 03 02 01   5 4 3 2 1

Library of Congress Cataloging-in-Publication Data

Loew, Patty.
Indian nations of Wisconsin : histories of endurance and renewal / Patty Loew.
p.   cm.
Includes bibliographical references and index.
ISBN 0-87020-335-5 (clothbound)
ISBN 0-87020-332-0 (paperbound)
1. Indians of North America—Wisconsin—History. 2. Indians of North America—Wisconsin—Social life and customs. I. Title.
E78.W8 L64 2001
977.5'00497—dc21

2001020918

For my mother, Alice DeNomie Loew,

and the DeNomie family

Contents

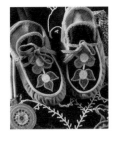  

Preface

Brandon Geshick, a Grass Dancer, performs at the annual St. Croix Wild Rice Pow Wow in Hertel.

Photo courtesy of St. Croix Band of Lake Superior Chippewa

On August 20, 1998, they came home. For the first time in nearly 175 years, the Sauk, Mesquakie, Dakota, and other Native Americans whose ancestors had been removed from Wisconsin—the Potawatomi from Kansas, Kickapoo from Oklahoma, and Winnebago now living in Nebraska—danced together in their ancestral homelands. Along with the tribes who remained in Wisconsin—the Ho-Chunk (related to the Nebraska Winnebago), Menominee, Ojibwe, Potawatomi, Mohican, Oneida, and Brothertown—they celebrated their survival in the "New Dawn of Tradition Pow Wow" in Madison. As I waited with other traditional women's dancers to enter the arena during the grand entry, I had a deep sense of history about this remarkable event. Not since the 1825 grand council in Prairie du Chien had all the original inhabitants of Wisconsin come together. Tragically, that gathering had culminated in a treaty that presaged land cessions and removal orders—developments that would bring poverty of land and spirit to generations of Native Americans.

Initially, there had been talk among some Wisconsin tribes about boycotting the New Dawn Pow Wow. Promoted as a "Sesquicentennial" event, the gathering raised the hackles of some tribal members. Native Americans asked how anyone could expect them to "celebrate" 150 years of Wisconsin statehood when it obviously came at the expense of their land and the erosion of their political rights. In the end, however,

Old meets new. Jingle Dancers perform in exhibition under the shadow of a giant television monitor at the New Dawn of Tradition Pow Wow, August 1998.

Photo courtesy of Great Lakes Inter-Tribal Council

most tribal members decided to view the week—devoted as it was to Wisconsin history and culture—as an opportunity to educate the white residents of this state about the injustices and triumphs of Indian people in Wisconsin. They chose to view it not as a commemoration of Wisconsin statehood, but as a celebration of Native American survival.

A year before the pow wow, the Great Lakes Intertribal Council, an umbrella organization representing the eleven federally recognized tribes in Wisconsin, asked me to research and write text for a large, walk-through public history exhibit on Indian nations in the state. The exhibit was to be displayed during the Folklife Festival, which was scheduled to coincide with the sesquicentennial celebration. The timing was excellent: I was preparing a seminar on Wisconsin Indians as part of my teaching fellowship in the History Department and American Indian Studies Program at the University of Wisconsin–Madison. Although I had done a fair amount of research on the Ojibwe for my Ph.D. dissertation, I knew little about the histories of other Indian cultures. I thought the experience would help me develop my seminar and nourish my personal interest in Native cultures. Over the next year, I met with tribal historians and directors of language and culture in each of the twelve Indian communities. The stories they shared with me and the materials they recommended formed the basis of the exhibit, the core of my lectures, and the genesis of this book.

As a member of the Bad River Band of Lake Superior Ojibwe, I have been frustrated by many of the books about the First People of this area. So often, Native history is filtered through white sources: missionary accounts, traders' journals, and government documents. Certainly these have been helpful in reconstructing the past, but frequently Native voices have been absent from their own histories. In this book, I have attempted to use as many Native sources as possible: speeches delivered by chiefs during treaty negotiations, origin stories, songs, legends, cave paintings, Native newspapers, and so on. I have tried to refer to the Native people as they refer to themselves. For example, for the Five Nations Confederacy I use the term *Haudenosaunee* instead of *Iroquois*—a derogatory term coined by an Algonquian-speaking tribe unfriendly to the Oneida. Other tribal terms include *Mesquakie* instead of *Fox* and *Anishinabe* or *Ojibwe* instead of *Chippewa*. Although the Ho-Chunk did not formally change their name from Winnebago until the end of the twentieth century, for purposes of simplicity and consistency I refer to them throughout their history as *Ho-Chunk*.

This is by no means an exhaustive study of the tribes in the state. It is my earnest attempt, however, to explore Wisconsin's rich native heritage in a collection of compact tribal histories. Therefore I confined my discussion to the twelve Indian nations—the Ho-Chunk, Menominee, Potawatomi, Oneida, Mohican, Brothertown, and six bands of Ojibwe—whose presence predated Wisconsin statehood and who have maintained a continuous residence here. The Dakota, Sauk, Mesquakie, Mascouten, and Kickapoo and Milwaukee's urban Indian population are important topics for further study.

Although I have combined the very early histories and fur trade experiences of the tribes into single narratives, I have organized subsequent chapters to emphasize the uniqueness of each Indian community. I discuss in a single chapter the politically autonomous Ojibwe bands, who shared a common history until 1854. The Brothertown Indians, who are not a federally recognized tribe, are presented in the chapter about the Mohicans, the tribe with whom they migrated to Wisconsin. From an organizational perspective, I thought it was important for the reader to understand that each tribe is culturally distinct, with its own language, ontology, and history. As much as possible, I have tried to include events and sociopolitical movements that remind us that the Indian nations residing in Wisconsin related not only to white policies and pressures but to each other as well.

This book was much more difficult to write than I ever imagined. I was asked to write a "history book," which carried with it certain expectations that the book I delivered would "look" like a history book, that it would include dates and documented "facts" arranged chronologically. But Native people tend to organize their histories thematically, with stories unfolding in a circular fashion. Time is relative and sometimes incidental. On an early version of this manuscript, one of my editors noted, "Could you be more precise about the time frame here? Would you say they moved their villages every five years? Ten years?" I made the change. Later, one of my Mohican readers gently scolded me: "That's so *white*," she told me. "Why don't you just say: 'as often as necessary.'" Of course, she was right. Although I have tried to avoid such references, some blurring of interpretation is

Traditional Oneida cornhusk dolls.

Photo courtesy of Oneida Nation

probably inevitable in a manuscript written by someone of mixed ancestry. It is with affection and good intentions that I offer this book.

. . . .

I am indebted to the tribal historians, elders, and friends in Wisconsin, some of whom not only shared their knowledge for the history project but also read portions of this manuscript, corrected errors, and suggested ways to improve it. Any mistakes in the book or errors of judgment are my fault, not theirs. In particular, I would like to thank Randy Tallmadge, Bernadine Tallmadge, and Ken Funmaker, Jr., of the Ho-Chunk Nation; Dr. Carol Cornelius and Loretta Metoxen in Oneida; June Ezold of the Brothertown Indians; Clarice Ritchie, Jim Thunder, and Billy Daniels in Potawatomi Country; Dorothy Davids, Ruth Gudinas, Bernice Miller Pigeon, and the Stockbridge Munsee Historical Committee; and David Grignon, Dr. Verna Fowler, and Alan Caldwell in Menominee. I owe a special thank you to Ada Deer, whose American Indian Issues course—the first seminar I took in graduate school—lit my academic fires.

I would also like to thank and acknowledge the wise Native men, women, and friends of my own nation who have guided my pen and spirit: Eddie Benton-Banai, Jim Schlender, Eugene Begay, and Paul DeMain at Lac Courte Oreilles; Gene Connor at St. Croix; the late Walt Bresette at Red Cliff; Tinker Schuman, Joe Chosa, George Brown, Jr., Nick Hockings, Peggy Grinvalsky, and Marcus Guthrie at Lac du Flambeau; Joe Rose, Richard Ackley, and Dana Jackson at Bad River; Fred Ackley, Chuck Ackley, and Fran VanZile at Mole Lake; and Bob Birmingham, State Archeologist. I would also like to especially thank Dr. David Wrone, history professor at the University of Wisconsin–Stevens Point, and Dr. Robert Bieder of the School of Public and Environmental Affairs, Indiana University, for reading the entire manuscript and offering excellent advice and criticism. Thanks also to Jon Kasparek for photo research and to everyone who provided photographs, including Andy Connors, Indian Community School of Milwaukee; Susan Otto, Milwaukee Public Museum; and Barbara Blackdeer-MacKenzie, Ho-Chunk Nation.

I am grateful to Jerry Rayala and Gloria Cobb of the Great Lakes Intertribal Council and the Wisconsin Humanities Council for the opportunity to learn from the extraordinary keepers of Indian culture in this state. Finally, I am indebted to the Wisconsin Historical Society—and in particular, my mentor, James Danky, and my editors, Michael Stevens and Paul Hass—for suggesting this project and entrusting it to my care, and to Kent Calder and Kathryn Thompson for seeing it through to its completion. *Miigwech.*

① Early History

A thousand years ago, after carefully preparing red, black, and blue-gray paints, an artist sanded the walls of a rock shelter hidden in a stand of mixed hardwoods in present-day Iowa County. Satisfied that the "canvas" was properly prepared, the artist—a historian, really—began to record a remarkable story. The walls filled with painted turtles, thunderbirds, and a mythic hero who wore human heads as earrings. Supernatural athletic contests and "giant" slayings unfolded in pictographic detail.

Members of the modern Ho-Chunk Nation recognize this composition as the story of Red Horn, an ancient Ho-Chunk hero. This origin epic, told by generations of tribal members and preserved in a cave known today as Gottschall, testifies to the enduring power of the spoken word and the persistence of Native American oral tradition.[1] Gottschall also provides other clues to the pre-Columbian Ho-Chunk past. Along with the Red Horn paintings, the cave contains pottery shards of the Effigy Mound Builders, whose earthen works first appeared about 3,000 years ago, and unusual soils associated with sacred rituals of the Mississippians, whose agriculture-based economy and impressive trade networks emerged about 1,000 years ago. The connection between Ho-Chunk oral history and the physical evidence at Gottschall suggests that rather than being separate peoples, later cultures evolved from and intersected with earlier ones.

The Gottschall site, a place of obvious cultural and religious significance, is just one of more than one hundred rock art sites identified in Wisconsin, most of them in the Driftless Area of the southwestern part of the state. From simple

The Red Horn composite in Gottschall Cave, Iowa County, tells an ancient Ho-Chunk story of heroes and giants. The story may relate to the arrival of the Mississippian Culture to the area.

Drawing by Mary Steinhauer; used with permission of Robert Salzer, Beloit College

1

grooves and incised geometric designs to elaborate painted birds, animals, and human forms, these cave drawings may have been created for spiritual or sacred reasons, inspired by dreams, fasts, or rituals. Perhaps Native artists carved or painted these motifs to educate the young or commemorate the dead. It is likely that the ancestors of today's modern Indian nations used pictographs as mnemonic devices to help tribal members remember important events or complex ceremonies.[2]

The Anishinabe, or Ne shna bek, a political and spiritual alliance comprising the Ojibwe, Ottawa, and Potawatomi, recorded pictographs on birch bark scrolls to help initiates remember sacred songs and sequences of the Midewiwin, or Medicine Lodge ceremonies. Each character related to a phrase in the chant, which was repeated a number of times. The integration of animal, human, and spirit figures in these scrolls illustrates how intimately the Anishinabe synthesized the natural world with spiritual beliefs. Although most closely associated with this most important religious society, Anishinabe picture writing was also used in more ordinary affairs of the tribe. Indeed, it became the lingua franca of diplomacy and commerce among many Native peoples.[3]

Wampum was another way Native American tribes communicated. Although wampum belts sometimes contained other colors, they were primarily strings of purple and white beads made from quahog shells gathered in an area near present-day Long Island, New York. For some tribes, the color of the wampum had meaning: white meant peace; purple or red sometimes meant war; black denoted sorrow or something serious.[4] Indian nations routinely used wampum belts in diplomatic relations. For example, when the Potawatomi received a dispatch in the form of a wampum belt, they sometimes referred to it as the "mouth" of the sender. After the arrival of Europeans, wampum became a form of monetary exchange.

Along with other intriguing fragments of the past, rock art, picture writing, and wampum are useful in reconstructing the experiences of Native cultures before they encountered Europeans. It is a history that encompasses a vast expanse of time. Although anthropologists believe that humans have occupied the Great Lakes region for at least 12,000 years, contemporary tribal historians resist such efforts to date human occupation of the area. According to the origin stories of most Indian nations in Wisconsin, the tribes have been here "from the beginning of time."

Early Native Americans adapted to a landscape dramatically different than the one we recognize today. Twelve thousand years ago, at the end of the Ice Age, small communities of hunters and gatherers searched for food in coniferous forests that grew in the paths of the retreating glaciers. They encountered frag-

Deer Effigy Mound, a rare four-footed effigy, is contained in one of two mound groups preserved on the Mendota State Hospital grounds in Madison. Most animal effigies were sculpted with two legs, not four. The Mendota State Hospital mound cluster is one of the finest in the world. In addition to the Deer Mound, the group contains two panthers, two bears, and three bird mounds, including one with an original wingspan of over 624 feet.
WHi(X3)41717

ments of tundra, spongy plains, and large lakes. Over the next 5,000 years, they learned to shape copper into useful and ornamental objects that they could trade to other communities. They began to cultivate certain crops, such as beans, squash, sunflower, and corn, selecting and sowing seeds that had the most desirable characteristics.

Postglacial erosion, however, created wildly fluctuating lake and river levels. At various times until 1500 B.P. (Before Present), some of Wisconsin's landscape may have been an uninhabitable bog. Interestingly, the Ojibwe and Potawatomi recall a time long ago when the people forgot the teachings of the Midewiwin, the spiritual foundation of the Anishinabe, and as punishment were forced to leave their homes and travel east. Like nearly every other Great Lakes tribe, they tell stories about water once covering the earth.

In the Ojibwe story of Winneboozho and the Great Flood, for example, the Creator purified Mother Earth with water. Then Winneboozho—half spirit, half man—found himself, along with the animals, clinging to a log. Winneboozho and the animals took turns diving under the water to try to bring up some earth. After better divers failed, Muskrat gave his life in a successful effort to retrieve a few grains of sand. From that bit of matter, Winneboozho created a New World, which Turtle offered to carry on his back. In honor of Turtle's sacrifice, some Native people today refer to North America as Turtle Island.[5]

The Oneida have a similar story of how the world began. Their version, however, begins in the Sky World after the Tree of Life is uprooted, leaving a gaping hole between the sky and a watery world below it. Sky Woman's jealous husband pushes her into the hole, but as she falls, she manages to grab a twig from the Tree. Four white swans carry her safely to the watery world, where Muskrat dives to retrieve some earth and Turtle offers his back to hold the spreading world. With seeds from the Tree of Life, Sky Woman begins to plant and creates Mother Earth. Contemporary Native Americans believe that flood stories such as these

Thunderbird Petroglyph, Twin Bluffs. The thunderbird is one of the most consistent images in Wisconsin rock art. The Thunderbird Clan is the largest clan among the Ho-Chunk and a significant clan among the Menominee.
Photo by Charles Brown; WHi(X3)13365

are evidence that their ancestors occupied the Great Lakes Region during the end of the last Ice Age.[6]

Physical evidence of early human presence, such as stone tools, spear points, and pottery, along with campsites and refuse pits, also helps us to understand what life was like in ancient times. These fragments of the past suggest that the earliest Native people subsisted mainly on a diet of plants and small mammals—rabbits, raccoons, and squirrels—as well as larger ones such as deer and elk. From spear points embedded in the buried bones of now-extinct mammoth and mastodon, we also know they once hunted these larger mammals. They learned to supplement their diet with fish and freshwater clams and mussels.

From the stories and songs passed down to present generations of Native Americans, we can make inferences about the relationships early inhabitants had with the animals and plants that sustained them. The Ho-Chunk, for example, sing about their reverence for deer and a hill near present-day Black River Falls where their ancestors used to hunt. It was here that deer would beckon Ho-Chunk hunters by singing to them songs of love: "If he is there, let him come. If he is there, let him come," the deer would call. "An old man fasted there," the Ho-Chunk remember. "They took pity on him—that hill, the deer, and Earth-maker. Whatever that was sacred, they could bestow on him, they did." The hill remains a spiritual place where tribal members fast and pray.[7]

The Ojibwe's appreciation for animals is evident in Fisher Goes to the Sky-world, a story about four animals who stole the sun and brought seasons to the earth. In this story, Mother Earth was dark and cold because the Sky People had captured the sun and all its warmth. Fisher, aided by his friends, Otter, Lynx, and Wolverine, dug a hole into the Skyworld and tried to capture the sun. As the sun's rays escaped, the earth began to transform itself. The snow melted and plants and trees appeared. By the time the Sky People discovered Fisher, he and his friends had dug a hole large enough for the sun to warm the earth half the year. Such stories reinforce the notion that ancient Native people viewed animals not as inferior creatures intended solely for human exploitation, but as helper beings with their own spirits and purposes.[8]

Plants, too, are imbued with human qualities and presented as helper spirits in Native American songs and stories. Potawatomi oral tradition hints at the strong connection earlier Native people may have had to the plants that nourished them—especially corn. Five mysterious strangers visited a young woman who was spared after the Creator "lifted up the whole world and dropped it in a lake." The first visitor was tall and wore a green blanket, which turned into tobacco leaves. The second, who was short and round, rolled on the ground and became a pumpkin. The third and fourth visitors became beans and squash. The fifth was a handsome man whom the young woman married. After their wedding, the husband revealed himself to be the leader of the corn nation. Rain blessed their union and produced an abundance of growing things. "The woman and the corn chief gave thanks to the Good Spirit," the Potawatomi remembered, "and taught their children how to pray and offer their thanks for corn, pumpkin, beans, squash, and tobacco."[9]

Whereas non-Indian anthropologists explain the tribes' increasing reliance on agriculture as an evolution from hunting and gathering, some Native elders and historians view their origin stories as proof that they have always had agriculture. However, advocates of both theories agree that the preeminence of agriculture represented a marked change in community life. With a more reliable food supply, tribal populations increased and Native Americans began to live in larger, more permanent villages. They developed more sophisticated political structures and traded more extensively. They devoted more time to artistic and religious expression, evidenced by the pottery that began to emerge and the effigy mounds that began to dot the landscape.

About 2,500 years ago, Native people began constructing earthen effigies, including turtles, bears, and humans. Some of the mounds were massive. A bird effigy near Muscoda in present-day Richland County, for example, had a wingspan of more than a quarter mile. Although many of the effigies contained human remains, some did not. It is likely that water held a special attraction for mound builders, since many of the earthen effigies were located near lakes and rivers. Intriguingly, in southern Wisconsin some of the mound groups correspond to Ho-Chunk clan divisions: eagles and thunderbirds from the sky world and bears representing the earth world. Some mound clusters include water panthers, which are symbolic of the underground spirits. There is some evidence that the tails of panther effigies often point to underground springs—entrances to the underworld, in the Ho-Chunk oral tradition.

Some researchers surmise that these mounds are the key to understanding the cosmology of the culture that built them—the people the Ho-Chunk call "ancestors." There is speculation that mound groups may symbolize the clan structures of some contemporary tribes. Others suggest they may be gargantuan maps or, perhaps like the Mayan pyramids, calendrical or astronomical devices. There is no question that for the people who built them, these monumental cultural expressions were a form of communication.

About a thousand years ago, an entirely different cultural group entered the region. Unlike the mound builders, the Mississippians had not emerged from the Great Lakes area but rather had migrated to the region from the south. They belonged to a powerful nation of people whose principal city, Cahokia, near

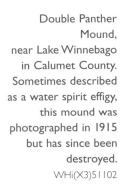

Double Panther Mound, near Lake Winnebago in Calumet County. Sometimes described as a water spirit effigy, this mound was photographed in 1915 but has since been destroyed.
WHi(X3)51102

present-day St. Louis, supported a population of at least 35,000. The Mississippians appear to have had a complex belief system that emphasized the interaction of the sacred and the secular.

The Mississippians developed an impressive trade network that extended from the Atlantic to the Rocky Mountains and from the Gulf of Mexico to the Great Lakes. Trade most likely led them to establish the village known today as Aztalan, considered one of Wisconsin's most significant archaeological sites, near present-day Lake Mills in Jefferson County. The palisade that surrounded the village suggests that these tall residents of Aztalan did not always live in harmony with their neighbors. Could they have been the "giants" slain in the Red Horn story?

From excavated refuse pits, we know that the residents of Aztalan grew considerable quantities of corn, beans, and squash. Their basic meat staple was venison, although they also ate duck, fish, and mussels. The site they chose for their village, along the west bank of the Crawfish River, provided lush bottomland for farming and easy access to fish and waterfowl. For some reason, however, Aztalan

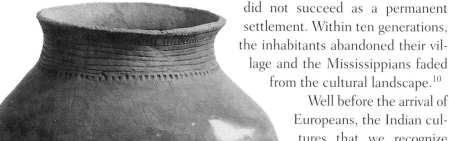

A Late Woodland pot excavated in the 1930s in Clam Lake, Burnett County.
Photo courtesy of Milwaukee Public Museum; neg. 71951

did not succeed as a permanent settlement. Within ten generations, the inhabitants abandoned their village and the Mississippians faded from the cultural landscape.[10]

Well before the arrival of Europeans, the Indian cultures that we recognize today lived in present-day Wisconsin: Siouan-speaking Ho-Chunk and Dakota (Sioux) in the north and west and Algonquian-speaking Menominee, Ojibwe, and Potawatomi in the northeast, central, and south. As could be expected from peoples sharing the same woodland environment, these tribes shared some characteristics. They lived in wigwams made from bent saplings sheathed with bark. They shared a similar diet. They hunted deer, rabbit, and waterfowl; fished for sturgeon, pike, lake trout, and catfish; gathered nuts, wild rice, berries, edible plants, and shellfish; and planted corn, beans, squash, tobacco, and sunflowers. Communities farther north, such as the Ojibwe, who were limited by shorter growing seasons, were less dependent upon agriculture than the Ho-Chunk and Menominee. Because of their reliance on hunting and trapping, the Ojibwe lived in smaller, more mobile bands. The Ho-Chunk and Menominee tended to inhabit larger villages.

Each tribe organized itself into clans, providing "a framework of government to give them strength and order," in the words of Edward Benton-Banai, a contemporary Anishinabe medicine man. In the Ojibwe O-do-daym-i-wan (clan system), there were seven original clans: Crane, Loon, Fish, Bear, Marten, Deer, and Bird. The Crane and Loon Clans contributed the chiefs, and their shared leadership provided important checks and balances. From the Fish Clan came the intellectuals and the mediators; from the Marten Clan, the warriors; from the Deer Clan, the poets. Bear Clan people served as protectors: some policed the village while others learned about medicines and used their knowledge to heal people. Finally, the Bird Clan provided the spiritual leaders. Marriage within a clan was forbidden.[11]

The Menominee and the Ho-Chunk divided their clans into two groups, representing either the earth or sky. Among the Menominee, the earth clans, including the Bear Clan, supplied the peace chiefs. The sky clans, such as the Eagle Clan, produced the war chiefs. In Ho-Chunk culture, the roles of the clans were reversed: sky clans were responsible for leadership during times of peace; earth clan chiefs led their communities during war.

The Ho-Chunk tell a story about the origin of the Buffalo Clan, an earth clan, which produced many fine warriors. A long time ago, an evil water spirit was terrorizing the Ho-Chunk who lived near Da Cesik—meaning Green Lake in east-central Wisconsin. Buffalo challenged the Water Spirit to a fight, and the two struggled in the cold, dark, "bottomless" lake. "The waters churned and churned and suddenly the Buffalo rose to the surface and lifted his head. He was victorious over the Water Spirit, and thus began the Buffalo Clan."[12]

It is worth noting that clan leaders, or chiefs, did not "rule" in the manner of

"Gathering Wild Rice."
Engraving after a drawing by
Seth Eastman, from the *American
Aboriginal Portfolio* by Mary H.
Eastman, 1853; WHi(X3)25013

European royalty but rather led by consent. Tribal members expected their chiefs to be generous and to put the interests of the community above their own interests. They especially appreciated leaders who were both shrewd negotiators and accomplished orators, useful skills in brokering treaties and forming alliances.

Many Indian nations created confederacies that still exist today. The best known of these is the Five Nations Confederacy, which includes the Oneida, one of the New York tribes that immigrated to Wisconsin Territory in the 1820s. Cen-

"Let the Great Spirits Soar," effigy tree stump sculpture in Madison, near Lake Monona, sculpted by Ho-Chunk artist Harry Whitehorse. This hackberry tree stands in a park filled with effigy mounds. After the tree was damaged by lightning, Whitehorse carved into it the figures of a wolf, eagle, bears, and a Native American. Photo courtesy of Robert Birmingham, WHS

turies earlier, the Oneida joined the Mohawk, Cayuga, Onondaga, and Seneca to form the Five Nations, or Great League. After the Tuscacora joined the League in the 1720s, it became known as the Six Nations Confederacy. According to oral tradition among Oneida still residing in New York, the League began during the month "when the corn was ripe and the grass was knee high" (August) and when the "sun went dark during the day" (a solar eclipse).

Based on the number of Thatatàlho (presiding chiefs) since the Confederacy was ratified, researchers at the University of Toledo estimated that the birth of the Confederacy occurred some time in the twelfth century. Of the eight solar

Two-Tailed Turtle Mound is located on Observatory Hill on the University of Wisconsin–Madison grounds. The turtle, also identified as a "Water Spirit," was one of several mounds in a group that included a bird effigy that spanned more than 130 feet, along with a panther and a linear mound. The bird and turtle effigies are all that remain.
WHi(X3)23678

eclipses that occurred during that time period, only one was visible in central New York during the month of August. In 1999, on the basis of this oral history, mnemonics, mathematics, and astronomical evidence, researchers concluded that the Oneida and their allies formally became the Five Nations Confederacy on August 31, 1142.[13] In Wisconsin, however, Carol Cornelius, a Wisconsin Oneida and tribal historian, cross-referenced the number of Thatatàlho to historical stories within her tribe's oral tradition and arrived at a much earlier date. Cornelius cautioned that Wisconsin Oneida do not accept any founding date, other than "a long time ago."[14]

For Native Americans, research that combines oral history, mnemonics, and physical evidence represents a new approach to reconstructing the past. Had archeologists not collaborated with Ho-Chunk elders, the priceless Red Horn composite at the Gottschall site might have remained an indecipherable mystery. The ancient songs, stories, and art of Native people are filled with symbolism and wisdom. In order to understand the cultural meaning of the people, places, and events that shaped their lives, we must not only *read* history, but also *listen* to it.

② European Arrivals

In the summer of 1634, the Ho-Chunk, Menominee, and Potawatomi near present-day Green Bay awoke to a strange sight: a light-skinned visitor who arrived at their villages by canoe, bearing gifts and displaying metal objects the Ho-Chunk later described as "thunder sticks." The visitor was Jean Nicolet, a French trader sent by the Governor of New France in North America, Samuel de Champlain, to negotiate peace between the Ho-Chunk and the Ottawa. Champlain hoped to expand his fur trade into the western Great Lakes area; however, hostilities between the Ho-Chunk and Ottawa had thwarted his plans. Nicolet's "thunder sticks" were, of course, firearms, and their introduction into Native culture would forever change the Indian nations.[1]

Some Native American prophecies had foretold the arrival of the "light-skinned hairy ones." The Ho-Chunk chiefs who met Nicolet in the village they called Moga-Shooch, or Red Banks, for example, welcomed him as their prophesies had instructed—by sprinkling tobacco on his head as a sign of honor and respect. Rumors that the pale-skinned people had actually arrived in eastern North America, however, likely had reached the inhabitants of the western Great Lakes long before Nicolet's visit. Indigenous trade networks, which kept the various tribes in regular contact, had existed for centuries.

Even before their actual arrival in the western Great Lakes region, Europeans had already touched the lives of the Native peoples. Intense competition between the French and their Algonquian friends and the Dutch and their Five Nations allies had led to open warfare and caused massive migrations. Refugee tribes fleeing the violence steadily encroached upon the lands of the Ho-Chunk and Menominee. The Sauk, Mascouten, Potawatomi, and Kickapoo moved west and north from around the southern edge of Lake Michigan. The Ojibwe, Ottawa, Mesquakie (Fox), and Iroquois-speaking tribes outside the Five Nations Confederacy pressed westward along the northern boundaries of Ho-Chunk and Menominee territory. For the Ho-Chunk, these northern encroachments were es-

Jean Nicolet arrives at Mogo-Shooch (near present-day Green Bay) in 1634. Although Nicolet is credited with being the first white man to visit the area, there is evidence that Étienne Brûlé actually may have explored the upper Great Lakes more than a decade earlier.
Painting by E. W. Deming, 1904; WHi(X3)30553

pecially threatening, since the intrusions pushed them southward toward the enemy tribes of the Illinois Confederacy.[2]

The tension between the Ottawa and the Ho-Chunk was especially fierce. Sometime before Nicolet's arrival, the Ho-Chunk had killed a delegation of Ottawa that had attempted to explore trade possibilities. The antagonism may have stemmed from attempts by the Ottawa to trade with the Sioux and other tribes the Ho-Chunk considered enemies. Whatever promises Nicolet elicited from the indigenous people of the western Great Lakes, peace was shattered a year after his visit, and the Ho-Chunk and Menominee were plunged into a cycle of continuous warfare with the refugee Algonquian tribes. Disease, perhaps brought by Nicolet and his party, further crippled the two nations. Amid the chaos, the Ho-Chunk and Menominee suffered tremendous hardship.

In the years immediately following Nicolet's visit, the Ho-Chunk focused their attention on those they perceived to be the most immediate threat: the Mesquakie. One Ho-Chunk story tells of a massive war party that traveled by canoe across Lake Winnebago to attack the Mesquakie. A storm arose, and hundreds of Ho-Chunk warriors drowned. Fearing reprisal, three separate Ho-Chunk communities, a total of 12,000 people, drew together in a single village to defend themselves. Unfortunately, a "yellow sickness," as the Ho-Chunk described it, descended upon the village and claimed the lives of one-third of the Ho-Chunk population.[3]

Animosities between the Ho-Chunk and the Illinois Confederacy also escalated. During the 1640s, a major offensive by Confederated tribes resulted in the near destruction of the Ho-Chunk. In 1665, when the French fur traders Nicholas Perrot and Jesuit Claude-Jean Allouez arrived in Green Bay, along with four hundred members of a Huron-Ottawa trading party, they found only five hundred Ho-Chunk survivors in a village wracked by starvation and disease.

With less than ten percent of their pre-Nicolet population surviving these decades of war and disease, the Ho-Chunk approached Algonquian families and offered their sons and daughters as spouses. By extending kinship to those who had encroached on their territory, they were able to survive and begin the process of rebuilding their nation.

The Menominee, who were strong allies of the Ho-Chunk, experienced similar distress. The influx of refugee tribes after 1660 strained the resources of the area. The demands of an expanding population and constant warfare scattered and depleted the game. There were fights over fishing grounds. One such quarrel escalated into a regional war after the Menominee constructed fish traps on one of their rivers, preventing sturgeon from reaching Ojibwe villages located upstream. When their protests went unheeded, the Ojibwe attacked a large Menominee village. The Menominee, with help from the Sauk, Mesquakie, and Potawatomi, retaliated. This sporadic warfare between the Ojibwe and the Menominee reflected territorial encroachments and shifting alignments.[4]

The arrival of the French in the Great Lakes region did not have the same immediate effect that British and other European settlers had had on tribes in the East. Whereas the Massachusetts colonists wanted land for farming and viewed the indigenous tribes as nuisances, the French were primarily interested in trade and looked upon the Great Lakes tribes as potential partners. Some French trading families sent their sons to live in the communities of their Indian trading partners so that they could learn the language and establish kinship ties. There was a great deal of cultural absorption by the French, who adopted Native foods, medicines, dress, and customs. Voyageurs, the French traders who traveled along the waterways of the Great Lakes, adapted Native modes of transportation, such as snowshoes and canoes, to suit their needs. Many traders married Indian women and assimilated themselves into Native communities. Together, the French and their Indian allies created what came to be called a "Middle Ground," where a mutually accepted system of borrowed and blended customs emerged.[5] Today, hundreds of tribal members carry the surnames of early French traders—among them Grignon, Corbine, Denomie, and Cadotte—a reflection of how intertwined the two cultures became.

The introduction of European trade goods and the absorption of French culture profoundly affected the indigenous people of the Great Lakes as well. Initially, the change strengthened tribal identities. Tribes whose economies were tied to agriculture, such as the Ho-Chunk and Menominee, became better farmers with metal hoes, axes, and tools for clearing the land. Copper kettles, knives, and utensils made domestic chores more tolerable. Hunting tribes, including the Potawatomi and Ojibwe, became better hunters with flintlock rifles, lead ammunition, and metal traps. On the other hand, firearms made warfare deadlier and potentially more catastrophic.

The seductive nature of European goods created irresistible incentives for Native communities to embrace an economic system that essentially exploited them. The value of finished trade goods always exceeded the value of the raw materials needed to produce them. Indian hunters provided an ever-increasing supply of pelts in exchange for lesser quantities of the manufactured items they desired. It was a system that fostered dependency. Tribes that willingly embraced it ultimately discovered that it depleted their natural resources and impoverished their people.

The demand for fur produced fundamental changes in both intertribal and intratribal relationships. When Indian hunters depleted the supply of fur-bearing animals in their own areas, they sometimes encroached on the hunting grounds of neighboring tribes. This produced friction and sometimes outright skirmishing. The political and social structures of Indian communities evolved to accommodate this new emphasis on hunting. Tribes that may have lived in larger villages prior to European contact, such as the Ho-Chunk and Potawatomi, separated into smaller bands in order to track game and harvest pelts more efficiently.

These changes had a pronounced effect on the role of Native women. The absence of male hunters for longer periods of time meant that women in larger communities, whose hunter husbands ranged far from home, undoubtedly found themselves doing more work—constructing and repairing lodges, gathering firewood, butchering game, and similar heavy work in which they usually were assisted by men. With most of the village men away, women had a greater responsibility in providing food for their families. Agriculture became more

Menominee sugaring camp.

Engraving by Mary Irvin Wright, circa 1896; WHi(X3)19690

important. In addition to planting and gathering, women and children probably engaged in more subsistence hunting and fishing.

Women whose tribes fragmented into smaller bands, and extended family units may have seen their political influence diminish. According to Ne shna bek oral tradition, each Potawatomi village had a woman's council, or W'okamakwe, made up of the eldest sisters of the male clan chiefs. These "honored women" were expected to lead their clan families "in paths of goodness" or be impeached and stripped of any power. New laws went first to the W'okamakwe and then to the men's council.[6]

After European contact, Potawatomi men relied less on female counsel. With the primary focus on hunting, decision making most likely fell to the leaders of these hunting expeditions—traditionally men, upon whom the safety and survival of the smaller bands depended. Furthermore, European notions about gender roles influenced the Indians with whom they traded. Exploration, trade, and politics were the domain of men in European societies. French traders expected to deal with Native men, not women.

From the French perspective, the tribes' loosely organized political structures were exasperating. There were no kings among the tribes of the Great Lakes, and no central authorities with whom political and economic power resided. Tribal chiefs and headmen, chosen on the basis of heredity or proven experience, led by consent, not by coercion. With no single entity authorized to speak for Indian communities, the French sometimes took to designating their own Indian "chiefs." In a pattern adopted by the English and later by the Americans, French traders staged ceremonies and presented flags and medals to Indians based on their friendliness and their ability to provide furs. By favoring these individuals with attention and giving them trade goods that could be distributed to other members of the tribe, the French undermined the basic political structures of tribes. This practice created deep divisions within the tribes, producing, in the words of one nineteenth-century Ojibwe historian, "jealousies and heart-burnings."[7]

The introduction of alcohol to Indian communities was another debilitating aspect of the fur trade. Simon Pokagon, a Potawatomi chief, described its arrival in his village as "the midnight of my soul." Fermented beverages were previously unknown to the tribes of the Great Lakes. French traders quickly exploited the weakness some Indians had for whiskey and rum and used it to gain advantage in trade negotiations. Pokagon, who lost two children to alcohol, asked how a race that had accomplished so much could have unleashed "'tchi-maw-tchi gi-go'— that great devil-fish upon the sea of human life."[8] In some cases, alcohol intensified the problems created by the need to accommodate a new economic system. Its effect was an increase in abuse, neglect, and violence. In other cases, alcohol dulled the pain of population losses resulting from disease and warfare associated with the fur trade. Although drunkenness in Indian villages was probably no more intense or frequent than it was in white communities on the frontier, alcohol, like the fur trade itself, fostered dependency among Native Americans.

In addition to European trade goods, the introduction of Christianity had profound effects on Native cultures. In 1661, Father René Menard, an itinerant Jesuit missionary, ventured into the Chequamegon Bay area with Huron and Ottawa fleeing from the Haudenosaunee. Although Menard died before completing his mission, four years later another Jesuit, Father Claude Allouez, arrived at La Pointe on present-day Madeline Island and established the Saint Esprit Mission for the Ojibwe. In 1671, Allouez also founded the St. Francis Xavier Mission on the Oconto River to serve the Menominee, Ho-Chunk, Sauk, Mesquakie, and Potawatomi.[9]

The Jesuits achieved varying success in converting the Great Lakes tribes to Catholicism. Disease, warfare, and chaotic change in the late seventeenth century made tribal members vulnerable to Christian promises of salvation and deliverance from sorrow, especially when traditional medicines often proved powerless against European diseases. Even as epidemics raged through Indian villages and devastated entire communities, the Jesuits, with their European immunities, often stayed healthy.

The Ojibwe had mixed feelings about the Muk-a-day-i-ko-na-yayg, or "Black Coats," as they called the Jesuits. At times they considered them to be helpful.

In 1665, the Jesuits established Saint Esprit Mission on the shores of Chequamagon Bay, creating religious divisions between the Christian converts and adherents of the traditional Midewiwin religion.

"The Missionary," a wood engraving by H. F. Higby based on a Frederic Remington illustration published in *Harper's Monthly*, April 1892; WHi(X3)14540

For the most part, however, they found them less respectful of their ways than the French traders with whom they interacted. Anishinabe medicine man Edward Benton-Banai blamed the Jesuits for turning tribal members away from the Midewiwin, the traditional Medicine Lodge religion, and for promoting factionalism between the Christian and Mide followers. According to Banai, Christian Indians were encouraged to "resent and reject" those who followed the Midewiwin way.[10]

The collapse of the Huron Confederacy in 1649 had immediate consequences for the tribes of the Great Lakes. The Huron had acted as a middleman for the resident nations. The tribe's virtual annihilation by the Five Nations Confederacy left the French fur trade in shambles. The only option available to the Great Lakes tribes was to bring their furs to Montreal, a dangerous proposition that took them into areas controlled by the Five Nations. Only the Ojibwe, Ottawa, and Potawatomi attempted the difficult journey, usually organizing massive canoe flotillas that could fight their way past enemy warriors.

In 1659, the arrival of two unlicensed traders—Pierre Esprit Radisson and his brother-in-law, Médard Chouart, Sieur des Groseilliers, a French nobleman— offered the Great Lakes tribes a new trading opportunity. Radisson and Groseilliers paddled into Chequamegon Bay after exploring the south shore of Lake Superior and the Keweenaw Peninsula. Following a year of furious trading with the Lac du Flambeau and Lac Courte Oreilles Ojibwe and the Santee Sioux, they returned to Quebec, only to have their substantial cargo of furs and other trade items confiscated by the Crown. However, word of their success spread, and soon unlicensed traders were pouring into the Great Lakes region.

For the tribes, these *coureurs de bois*—"woods runners"—were a welcome relief. Their presence enabled Indian communities to conduct exchanges closer to home without exposing themselves to the Five Nations threat. For the French, however, the *coureurs de bois* represented a dilemma. On the one hand, they extended French influence into previously unexplored areas. On the other, they paid no royalties to the Crown. In addition, the Jesuits complained that the *coureurs de bois* indiscriminately supplied Indians with liquor and generally debauched them. A more serious concern, however, was that the uncontrolled trading they promoted created a glut of furs. This lowered prices and contributed to the overall economic and political instability of the area. When King Louis XIV of France officially forbade the tribes to trade with the *coureurs de bois*, Indian traders simply ignored the order.

The French responded by closing outlying forts and relocating their official traders to consolidated trading centers such as Detroit. They hoped this would entice their Indian partners living in Green Bay to move. Some of the refugee tribes did, in fact, resettle near Detroit, enabling the Menominee and Ho-Chunk to reoccupy the lands they had inhabited at the time of European contact. But overall, the French resettlement policy was a dismal failure. Relocation produced infighting among the tribes and opened the door to British traders, who were more than happy to fill the void left by the French exodus from the western Great Lakes.

In the 1740s, British traders began moving into the Ohio Valley. The shifting loyalties that marked intertribal and intratribal politics during the years of the French intensified with the arrival of the British. The French responded by building or reopening a string of forts, including one at Green Bay and another at Michilimackinac (present-day Mackinac Island).

Between 1753 and 1759, the French and their allies clashed with the British and their allies in what is known in America as the French and Indian Wars. Ultimately, the British prevailed when in 1759 General James Wolfe defeated the

Fort Mackinac, circa 1812. Mackinac, or Michilimackinac as it was originally known, was the site of two major battles involving pan-Indian forces. In 1763, under the ruse of a lacrosse game, Anishinabe warriors attacked and took the fort, hoping to return it to French rule. In 1812, Anishinabe supporting Tecumseh and his British allies led a successful attack against American forces at the fort.

From *The Pictorial Field-Book of the War of 1812* by Benson J. Lossing, 1869; WHi(X3)15057

main body of the French army outside Quebec. Montreal surrendered a year later. Although most of the Great Lakes Indian nations officially declared themselves neutral in the fighting, individual Indian warriors, especially Anishinabe, hired themselves out as mercenaries. Members of the Denomie family from the Ojibwe community at La Pointe, for example, were listed as scouts for French General Joseph de Montcalm's troops in the battle for Quebec.[11] Charles de Langlade, the son of a French trader and an Ottawa woman, was one of the strongest French allies. In 1752, Langlade led a force of Ojibwe, Potawatomi, and Ottawa against Old Briton, a Miami chief and British ally, at Pikawillany along the Miami River in Ohio. Three years later, Langlade and his warriors also ambushed and helped defeat General Edward Braddock's British army as it marched on Fort Duquesne, near present-day Pittsburgh.[12]

The tribes of the Great Lakes reacted differently to the arrival of the British. Among the Anishinabe, who enjoyed kinship and most-favored-nation trade status with the French, there was great uneasiness. Among the Menominee and Ho-Chunk, who resented the favoritism shown the Anishinabe and found the French trading system exasperatingly inefficient and disorganized, there was considerable optimism. The two factions did agree that English trade items were less expensive and generally of better quality than French items.

From the beginning, English trade practices were substantially different from those of their predecessors. Whereas the French lavished gifts upon their Indian partners, the British offered no such presents. Sir Jeffrey Amherst, the commander-in-chief of British Forces in North America who directed military actions from the East, dismissed gift-giving—an essential part of tribal culture—as bribery. Instead he adopted a diplomatic strategy based on fear and reprisal. The French had usually extended credit to their trading partners, supplying them with ammunition for hunting and food during particularly harsh winters. Amherst ordered the commanders of his western forts to intentionally keep the Indians short of ammunition. Further, he insisted that all trading be conducted inside the fort in order to control the exchange of alcohol, weapons, and ammunition. Amherst's high-handed decrees produced wholesale resentment in Indian communities. When Pontiac, the son of an Ottawa chief and an Ojibwe woman, organized a pan-Indian military effort to oust the British, all but the Menominee and Ho-Chunk nations in the western Great Lakes enthusiastically offered their support.

In April 1763, Pontiac organized a war council along the Aux Ecorces River attended by four hundred chiefs and warriors. They agreed that on a certain day in June, they would rise up in unison and attack the British forts in their areas, including Michilimackinac, a principal trading fort for the Great Lakes tribes. Beginning in early June, Indian warriors, including Ojibwe, Potawatomi, Sauk, and

Fort Crawford, in Prairie du Chien, was a major trading center for the Ho-Chunk, Menominee, Ojibwe, Potawatomi, Sauk, Mesquakie, and Dakota people.
WHS Archives, Album 12.24a, WHi(X3)2797

Mesquakie, rose up against fourteen British forts and eventually managed to take most of them. At Michilimackinac, the Ojibwe organized a lacrosse game outside the fort, ostensibly for the amusement of British troops inside the fort, who were celebrating the King's birthday. Posing as spectators and participants, the warriors had given their weapons to their women, who hid them inside their blankets and clothes. After the ball was launched toward the gates of the fort, the warriors grabbed their weapons, rushed in, and overwhelmed the garrison. Sixteen soldiers were killed outright and twelve others taken captive.[13] Elsewhere, confederated warriors lay siege to Forts Detroit and Pitt and forced the British to flee Fort Edward Augustus in Green Bay.

When the British abandoned their fort in Green Bay, they "entrusted" its care to the Menominee, a tribe that had no interest in seeing French influence restored in the area. Menominee warriors, who had been coerced into fighting for the French during the French and Indian Wars, returned with smallpox and ill will toward the French. During the winter of 1759, they revolted and killed twenty-two French soldiers. In retaliation, the French seized some of the warriors who had participated in the uprising and executed them in Montreal. As a result, the Menominee did not join Pontiac's Rebellion. In fact, after the Ojibwe captured Michilimackinac, the Menominee helped ransom British prisoners from the fort.

Although the rebellion failed to permanently oust the British, it did force important concessions. The British issued the Proclamation of 1763, which forbade their American colonists from settling west of the Appalachians. This decree, however, failed to stop westward expansion. The British Crown expanded trade, relaxed restrictions on the sale of guns and ammunition to the tribes, and restored the French practice of gift giving. At Michilimackinac, the British began using French traders to deal with the Ojibwe. The result was a gradual shift in Indian loyalties from the French to the British. By the time of the American Revolution (1775–1783) and the War of 1812, most of the Wisconsin tribes fought on the side of the British, not the Americans.[14]

③ Menominee

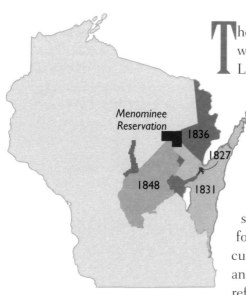

Menominee
Reservation
1836
1827
1848
1831

MENOMINEE

2001 population: 8,055
1854 Treaty: 236,548 acres
1856 Treaty: 232,400 acres
1961–1973: Tribal status
   terminated
1999: 236,548 acres (230,420
   tribally owned)

The history and identity of the Menominee people is rooted in the white pines and towering sugar maples of the western Great Lakes. The forest sustained the tribe before Europeans arrived on the continent, and to this day the forest continues to provide cultural and economic sustenance to the Menominee. As a present-day Menominee descendant explained, "We *are* the forest."[1] The struggle to preserve this critical resource, however, nearly cost the Menominee both their land and their identity as an Indian people.

The years following the arrival of the French in the mid-seventeenth century were ones of great change and adaptation for the Menominee. Tribal members experienced considerable cultural stress because of increased warfare, disease, and political and economic instability. Overhunting of Menominee land by refugee tribes fleeing the Five Nations strained the area's resources. The environmental pressure outsiders placed on the forest is a theme that would repeat itself throughout Menominee history.

The American Revolution brought more changes for the Menominee. Tribal members not only provided the British with canoes, furs, and other supplies, but also joined the British in battles against the Americans in New York, Ohio, Missouri, Pennsylvania, and Indiana.[2] Even after the Treaty of Paris (1783) transferred control of the region to the Americans, the British maintained their presence in Menominee country. Despite a series of Trade and Intercourse Acts between 1790 and 1802 that attempted to restrict commercial contact with tribes to traders licensed by the American government, few American traders ventured into Menominee country. British traders and the old resident French traders continued to conduct their business without interference from the new American government.

The Menominee Forest, one of the planet's healthiest forests, has sustained the Menominee for hundreds of years.
Courtesy of Wisconsin Conservation Dept.; WHi(X3)26181

Events taking place farther east, however, eventually drew the Menominee into the War of 1812. American settlers began trespassing on Indian lands in the Ohio Valley in violation of federal laws that forbade settlement west of the Appalachians. In response, Tecumseh, a Shawnee warrior, amassed a pan-Indian military alliance and began raiding the illegal settlements. Tecumseh argued that it was only a matter of time before the Americans threatened the nations of the Great Lakes as well. The Menominee, however, were convinced that war with the Americans was irrational and could not be won. As a result, the Menominee stayed neutral during these border wars (1783–1812). It was not until Tecumseh's battles merged with those of the British in the War of 1812 that the Menominee entered the fighting.[3]

In July 1812, about forty warriors, including the seventeen-year-old Oshkosh, joined British officer and trader Robert Dickson and a contingent of Ho-Chunk and Sioux in taking Fort Michilimackinac without firing a shot. After the war, and under the tutelage of the great Menominee war chief Tomah, Oshkosh became leader of the Bear Clan. He rose to prominence within his clan just as the Menominee began facing major land crises.

Pressure in the Oneida homeland led a Christianized group of New York Indians—the Oneida, Stockbridge, Munsee, and Brothertown—to seek land in the west. In August 1821, they approached the Menominee and Ho-Chunk Nations and expressed interest in the territory of the two tribes. Under pressure from the American government, the Menominee and Ho-Chunk agreed to "joint tenancy" with the New York tribes along an eighteen-mile strip straddling the Fox River north of Lake Winnebago. In September 1822, during a second council between the Menominee and the New York Indians, negotiators purportedly increased the size of the land in question to the "whole of the Menominee country East and North of Winnebago Lake." In exchange for this right to share the land, the New York tribes offered the Menominee five thousand dollars in goods.

There are conflicting accounts of the events surrounding the negotiations between the Menominee and the New York Indians. Some believe that the Menominee actually invited the New York Indians to join them in an effort to protect and hold their land. As evidence, they offer congressional documents revealing that in 1820, French and mixed-blood traders had executed a major land grab, securing title to more than seventy-five square miles of Menominee land along the Fox River south of Green Bay. According to this version, Menominee clan chiefs assumed that the New York Indians, who had considerable legal experience in land disputes with whites, might provide not only strength in numbers but also expertise.

A less charitable interpretation is that the New York Indians, some of whom had been educated in white schools, used their sophisticated understanding

Tecumseh, Shawnee war leader and brother of Tenskwatawa, the Shawnee Prophet. After the United States declared war on Great Britain in 1812, the Menominee joined Tecumseh's military alliance.
Courtesy of the Field Museum of Natural History, Chicago

of property issues to unfair advantage in the Menominee land negotiations. Although the Menominee understood the agreements to mean that they would *share* land with the New York Indians—a concept compatible with their own traditional view of the land—white negotiators increasingly framed the arrangement as a land *cession*. Furthermore, the Menominee argued that land cessions arranged by anyone other than an agent authorized by the President of the United States violated both the U.S. Constitution and the Trade and Intercourse Acts. The arrival of a small group of Stockbridge Indians in 1822 and a sizable contingent of Oneida, Mohican, and Brothertown immigrants in 1824 produced considerable anxiety among the Menominee.

In 1825, U.S. officials invited all the tribes residing in present-day Wisconsin to a Grand Council at Prairie du Chien. They explained the gathering as an opportunity to sign a "peace and friendship" treaty that would end intertribal warfare in the region, most notably between the Ojibwe and the Dakota. In the process, the leaders of the attending nations were pressured to declare their boundaries, an exercise that proved to be the crucial first step in alienating the tribes from their land. Within a few years of the treaty, U.S. negotiators began approaching each nation to arrange land cessions.

The Menominee were reluctant to declare their boundaries, not only because of the disputed Oneida land sale, but also because of a vacuum in leadership. "It is a long time since we have had any Chief," they informed the commissioners.[4] Because the Menominee were underrepresented at the Council (four times as many Ojibwe as Menominee signed the treaty), U.S. officials agreed to discuss the boundaries issues with them again at Butte des Morts two years later. In the meantime, Commissioner Lewis Cass asked the Menominee to designate a chief with whom Cass could conduct the negotiations, informing them that he too intended to select a chief. Cass eventually settled upon Oshkosh, grandson of Cha-wa-non (whom whites called "the Old King") and protégé of Tomah, a powerful war leader.

In 1827, at Butte des Morts, the Menominee agreed to boundaries between their land and that of the Ojibwe. Later, in the Treaty of 1831, the Menominee were pressured into giving up a portion of that land to be set aside for the New York Indians. The Scratcher (misidentified as Chief Grizzly Bear in the minutes of the proceedings), a celebrated speaker of the Menominee Council, told the commissioners that his people understood that the Oneida had come "not to purchase land, but to procure the grant of a small piece to sit down upon, that they might live with us like brothers."[5] Unwilling to come to terms with the New York Indian claims, the Menominee delegation agreed to allow President John Quincy Adams to settle the disputed claim.

Later that year, when fighting broke out between white settlers and a band of Ho-Chunk led by Red Bird, a company of Menominee, along with some Onei-

da and Stockbridge Indians, served with the U.S. Army. A decision on whether the Menominee would engage their traditional allies was averted when the Ho-Chunk surrendered Red Bird to U.S. officials. The next Menominee service to the Americans came in 1832 when Black Hawk's band of Sauk Indians resisted resettlement and attempted to return to their homes in present-day Illinois. A battalion of 250 Menominee, under the leadership of Feather Shedder, protected the white citizens of Green Bay who lived in fear of a Sauk attack.

Oshkosh, Menominee Clan leader and protégé of the war chief Tomah. Oshkosh was one of the principal negotiators during the crisis years when federal officials threatened to remove the Menominee to lands west of the Mississippi.

Painting by Samuel Marsden Brookes; WHS Museum Collections 42.59; WHi(X3)41832

Oshkosh, meanwhile, had narrowly avoided life in prison. In 1830, he found himself facing murder charges in a white court. He and two other Menominee were accused of fatally stabbing a Pawnee Indian who had killed a member of the Menominee Nation. Menominee law held that Oshkosh was within his rights to take the man's life, but a territorial jury found him guilty of manslaughter. Judge James Doty, however, reviewed the case, reasoned that Menominee law should apply on Menominee land, and ordered that all charges be dropped. Doty, who also represented the American Fur Company, may have had ulterior motives in freeing Oshkosh. The company was very interested in acquiring Menominee land. Given his prominence within the Bear Clan, Oshkosh represented someone who Doty perceived might help the company in that effort.[6] Despite government efforts to install Oshkosh as principal chief with the authority to speak for the entire tribe, the Menominee resisted such attempts and continued to rely upon a council of clan leaders to guide them through a difficult decade.

Following the Treaty at Butte des Morts, pressure on the Menominee to give up land escalated. In 1831, tribal representatives signed a treaty in Washington, D.C., in which the Menominee ceded three million acres in exchange for $146,500 over twelve years. The area ceded included 500,000 acres "for the benefit of the New York Indians." The U.S. Senate, however, amended the treaty by adding an article that changed the boundary lines of the land set aside for the New York Indians. The Menominee refused to ratify the new document, arguing that the changes adversely affected their trade routes. Negotiators redrew the boundary lines, and in 1832 the Menominee signed the amended treaty.[7]

Four years later, the Menominee were pressured into ceding the eastern half of their remaining territory. In 1848 they were forced to cede the remaining western half. As Wisconsin statehood loomed, the Menominee were ordered to exchange their lands for a small reservation in Minnesota. Two years later, a group of Menominee clan leaders, including Oshkosh, reluctantly led an exploratory expedition to the Crow Wing River area in Minnesota. When they returned, they told tribal members that Crow Wing was unsuitable for the Menominee. Oshkosh announced that "the poorest region in Wisconsin was better than the Crow Wing," adding that constant fighting between the Dakota and Ojibwe threatened the safety of his people.[8] He and other clan leaders followed their visit to the Crow Wing area with a trip to Washington, during which they met with President Millard Fillmore and persuaded him to temporarily rescind the removal order. Over the next several years, the Menominee council filed petitions and used delaying tactics to resist removal. The tribe's persistence paid off. In the Treaty of 1854, the Menominee were allowed to reserve 276,000 densely forested acres along the Wolf and Oconto Rivers for a permanent home.[9]

Grizzly Bear, Menominee Clan leader and negotiator in the Menominee treaties.
Sketch by George Catlin, circa 1831.
Courtesy of Smithsonian American Art Museum, DC/Art Resource

After the Menominee were settled, they bought a squatter's sawmill on tribal land and began cutting small amounts of timber. Oral history is clear on the Menominee's approach. Their elders advised them to begin selectively cutting mature trees in the east, working toward the west. When they reached the reservation boundaries, the trees in the east would be ready for them to harvest again.

In 1871, the Secretary of the Interior approved a plan to expand and enhance commercial logging on the Menominee Reservation. The tribe began selling logs to sawmills outside the reservation.[10] The profitability of their sawmill allowed the Menominee to escape the fate of other Wisconsin tribes, whose lands were divided and privatized under the General Allotment Act of 1887. Allotment was part of a multifaceted government effort to assimilate Indians and economically exploit Native lands and resources. Government officials expected that as forest-

Logging on the
Menominee
Reservation, 1909.
WHi(X3)33623

ed lands were cleared, Indians would turn to farming and become self-sufficient. Government officials decided not to allot the Menominee reservation because the logging operation had already brought the tribe a measure of self-sufficiency.

Tribal members could not escape the government's other efforts to assimilate them. Indian agents had absolute authority over the education of Indian children. The Browning Ruling, a policy in effect from 1896 to 1902, explicitly stated that "Indian parents have no right to designate which school their children shall attend."[11] Some Menominee children were sent to government boarding schools in Wisconsin—Lac du Flambeau, Tomah, and Hayward—and as far away as Flandreau, South Dakota, and Carlisle, Pennsylvania. Others remained on the reservation and attended St. Joseph's Catholic School in Keshena. In some schools, educators forbid Menominee from speaking their native language or engaging in Menominee cultural practices. The imposition of white culture upon entire generations of Menominee caused profound cultural confusion and contributed to a deep sense of loss that continues to this day.

At the turn of the twentieth century, some Menominee continued to hunt, fish, and gather on a subsistence basis. However, many tribal members found jobs in the timber industry. By 1905, at an annual cut rate of 20 million board feet, the Menominee had harvested nearly 300 million board feet of timber. That year, however, a tornado blew down 40 million board feet. The Menominee, accustomed to floating white pine down the Wolf River to private sawmills in the area, could not do this with much of the blown-down timber, which consisted primarily of hardwood trees that would not float. To better enable the Menominee to process the extra logs, Congress authorized construction of three temporary sawmills on reservation land. The tribe was supposed to get bids from outsiders to build the mills, which the Menominee would operate themselves. The bids, however, failed to materialize. Two years later the sapwood was gone and the hardwoods had begun to decay.[12]

At the request of the Menominee, U.S. Senator Robert M. La Follette of Wisconsin successfully introduced a bill and gained passage of legislation directing the U.S. Forest Service, in cooperation with the Interior Department, to organize logging on the Menominee Reservation on a sustained yield basis. La Follette's legislation was consistent with the tribe's own vision. It was designed to ensure that the Menominee would continue to selectively cut only mature trees—an estimated 20 million board feet annually—along with the trees affected by the blow-down.

Sustainable forestry was a radically different approach to forest management than the philosophy of clear-cutting advocated by commercial loggers and most government foresters. Forest Service officials, who "knew nothing and cared less" about selective cutting, simply ignored La Follette's mandate.[13] Instead of constructing three small temporary mills that could be dismantled after the downed timber was logged, forestry officials built one expensive sawmill capable of sawing 40 million board feet annually—twice the volume authorized by Congress.

As a result, the Menominee were saddled with an oversized sawmill (paid for with tribal funds), which in order to be profitable had to process twice as much timber as tribal foresters thought appropriate. Despite the protests of the tribe and local foresters appointed by the Interior Secretary, entire sections of the Menominee Forest were clear-cut. The practice continued until 1926, when the Interior Department wrenched control of the Menominee logging operations from the Forest Service. Over the next twelve years, cutting was scaled back from seventy percent of the salable timber to just thirty percent.

In 1934, the Menominee filed suit in the U.S. Court of Claims, alleging that the Forest Service had mismanaged their resource. Evidence revealed that more than ten percent of the reservation—half a billion board feet of timber—had been clear-cut. Furthermore, according to expert witnesses called by the tribe, federal foresters had failed to replant the cutover as promised and "abandoned" proper slash disposal. This "indifference" led to forest fires that further damaged the resource. The court awarded the Menominee Nation $8.5 million.

This judgment, which finally came in 1952, made the Menominee attractive candidates for "termination," an ill-conceived federal effort of the 1950s to dismantle the reservation system. Termination reflected a dramatic departure from Indian policy of the previous fifteen years. Under the 1934 Indian "New Deal," assimilation programs, such as allotment, had ended. Most Indian boarding schools had closed. Many Indian nations, including the Menominee, reorganized their tribal governments and adopted constitutions. Indian self-determination had its critics, however, who wanted to "free" Indian people from government paternalism and integrate them into mainstream society. Termination also "freed" the government from the cost of its treaty obligations to protect Indian people and their property.[14]

In 1953, Congress passed House Concurrent Resolution 108, which laid out the goals of termination and its companion policy, "relocation," which was intended to move Indian people from rural reservations to urban areas. Among the enticements were job training programs and housing assistance. Unfortunately, most Menominee who opted for relocation received only one-way bus tickets to Chicago, Milwaukee, or St. Paul. Inevitably, without proper support systems, most languished in these cities.

The leading proponent of termination, Senator Arthur Watkins of Utah, searched for tribes that might have the financial wherewithal to fend for themselves. By white standards, the Menominee were poor. However, with $10 million in their trust account, the Menominee were one of the wealthiest tribes in the country.

The Menominee tribal council voted to distribute a portion of the claims settlement—$1,500—to each member of the tribe. After Wisconsin Congressman Melvin Laird and Senator Joseph R. McCarthy introduced a bill in Congress authorizing the Interior Department to set aside the money for that purpose, Watkins, who sat on the Senate Committee on the Interior, held up the appropriation, demanding that the Menominee first submit a termination plan. Watkins pressured the Menominee to support termination, telling them that if they did not agree to the principle, within three years Congress would terminate them anyway. During a visit to Wisconsin, the senator insisted on a tribal vote that tied the issue of termination to the per capita payment. Fewer than six percent of the 3,200 tribal members were at the meeting. Of the 174 voters who cast ballots, only five voted against termination. Two days later, when they understood the full implications of termination, however, the Menominee took another vote and this time voted unanimously to oppose termination.[15] Unfortunately, Congress ignored the second vote and in 1954 passed Public Law 399, better known as the Menominee Termination Act.

In an effort to preserve their tribal identity and their land base, the Menominee voted to become a separate county. In July 1959, Governor Gaylord Nelson signed a bill creating Menominee County. After the per capita payments were made, the tribe had $7 million with which to create a county infrastructure, including roads, schools, law enforcement, courts, parks, and recreation. By 1961, when the tribe was officially terminated, this so-called "wealthy" tribe was losing about a quarter million dollars a year and had become the poorest among Wisconsin's seventy-two counties.

The Menominee, with plenty of solicited and unsolicited help from state and federal legislators, BIA representatives, and tribal attorneys, created Menominee Enterprises Incorporated (MEI) to oversee the tribe's financial interests. Each tribal member received one hundred shares in MEI, which featured a complicated organizational structure including a board of directors and two trusts. The Voting Trust, comprising four Menominee and three non-Indians, elected the MEI Board of Directors. The Menominee Assistance Trust held the proxy votes for children, incompetent tribal members, and prisoners. The Bureau of Indian Affairs appointed First Wisconsin Trust Company as guardian of the Assistance Trust, for which it received $214,000 annually. First Wisconsin represented nearly half the certificates and always voted its shares as a bloc. The resulting structure ensured that the Menominee would not control their own tribal operations.

Termination carried a tremendous quality-of-life cost. Previously, the Menominee had provided one hundred percent of the funding for a Catholic hospital on the reservation. Shortly after termination, the Voting Trust ordered the hospital closed, and tribal members were without medical care. The tribe had always over-employed its mill, believing it was more important to provide jobs than increase profits. Under a board of directors controlled by white financial interests, the emphasis shifted to the bottom line. In order to become more efficient and profitable, MEI began modernizing equipment and laying off workers. Menominee began to leave the reservation for jobs in the city, an exodus that further diminished the tribe's tax base. The board of directors looked to different solutions to attack the tribe's insolvency. It voted to lease some of the tribe's finest

land along the Wolf River to the state of Wisconsin for a public campground and to offer long-term leases to tourists for summer homes.[16]

A grassroots activist group, Determination of Rights and Unity for Menominee Shareholders (DRUMS), emerged in the late 1960s and began to educate tribal members about the trust situation and the need to change the financial structure of MEI. It sent a Menominee student, Ada Deer—who was then at the University of Wisconsin and who later became Assistant Secretary of the Interior—to Washington to lobby Congress in the hopes of repealing termination and restoring the tribe.

In 1968, MEI announced plans to create a lake and sell lots to non-Indians. After the developer of the so-called "Legend Lake" project promised MEI $6 million in sales and $2 million in shared profits, DRUMS took its protests public. DRUMS members organized a march from Keshena to the state capitol in Madison. They filed suits in federal court claiming that the dams required for the

project would inundate streams and marshes and adversely affect wildlife habitat. Menominee elders lay down along the highway leading to the real estate office to prevent land sales. In 1972, after dozens of homesites had already been sold, MEI agreed to terminate the Legend Lake project. A year later, Congress passed the Menominee Restoration Bill, which restored official status to the tribe.

On New Year's Eve, 1974, the tribe found itself ill-equipped to deal with a crisis that unfolded at an abandoned Catholic facility in Gresham. A group calling itself the Menominee Warrior Society muscled its way past a caretaker into the Alexian Brothers Novitiate and demanded that it be turned over to the Menominee tribe for use as a hospital. Still grappling with post-termination issues, the Menominee had not yet had time to elect council members. After an elected Restoration Committee publicly denounced the takeover as illegal, Governor Patrick J. Lucey called out the National Guard, which surrounded the facility. Eventually the warriors withdrew after a thirty-four-day standoff, but the incident created hard feelings and divisions within the Menominee, some of which have still not healed.[17]

The Menominee have struggled to rebuild after the disastrous effects of termination. Following passage of the National Indian Gaming Act in 1988, the Menominee opened a casino, bingo, and hotel complex in Keshena. With gaming dollars, they have built a new health clinic and schools and have taken over some welfare programs previously administered by the state and federal governments. They are one of two Indian nations in Wisconsin to operate their own tribal community college: the College of the Menominee Nation, which educates both Native and non-Native students.

Compared to the neighboring tribes in Wisconsin, the Menominee Nation has been able to assert more sovereign control over its reservation. In 1973, when the Menominee received fed-

During the late 1960s and early 1970s, Menominee tribal members staged protests and marches in an effort to regain tribal control of Menominee Enterprises Incorporated and halt the sale of Menominee land.

Milwaukee Journal photo; © Journal Sentinel, Inc.

National Guard troops stand ready outside the Alexian Brothers Novitiate in Gresham. On December 31, 1974, the Menominee Warrior Society took over the abandoned facility and occupied it for thirty-four days before negotiating a withdrawal.
WHi(X3)35383

eral recognition as a tribe, they successfully petitioned Congress to be exempt from Public Law 280, a measure passed in 1952 that transferred civil and some criminal jurisdiction from the federal government to five states with large Indian populations, including Wisconsin. The Menominee reasoned that, as a result of termination, they already had police and courts equipped to handle disputes. Consequently, tribal police or federal marshals handle crimes involving tribal members on the Menominee Reservation. In contrast, Indians who commit crimes on all other reservations in Wisconsin fall under county and state jurisdiction.

Today the Menominee are marginally solvent, largely because of their gaming facilities and their forest, which they operate on a sustainable yield basis. Now that they manage the forest themselves, they have gone back to the advice of their elders and cut selectively east to west. The Menominee Forest, which has

Above: College of the Menominee Nation, Keshena.
Photo by Patty Loew

Right: John Teller teaches the Menominee language to kindergarten children at the Menominee Tribal School in Neopit.
Photo by Patty Loew

Below: The Wolf River, a federally designated Wild River, flows through the Menominee Reservation.
Photo courtesy of Great Lakes Intertribal Council

become a laboratory for sustainable forestry, is considered one of the most beautiful and healthy forests on earth. Forest managers from all over the world visit it, marveling at its diverse number of species and mixed ages, including four-hundred-year-old hemlocks. Recently, a space shuttle astronaut described a large green patch west of Lake Michigan that looked like a "jewel." His observation probably did not surprise the Menominee. It was their forest.

Ho-Chunk

Ho-Chunk communities

HO-CHUNK

2001 population: 6,065
1962: 554 acres
1978: 3,673 acres (individually owned homesteads)
1999: 4,325 acres (918 tribally owned)

The Ho-Chunk people express their remembered past in the songs, stories, effigy mounds, rock art, and place names that dot the landscape of their ancestral home. For thousands of years, the Ho-Chunk have lived in the western Great Lakes region, south and west of present-day Green Bay. The Ho-Chunk, or Ho-chungra, formerly were known as the Winnebago, which came from the Mesquakie word *Ouinipegouek,* meaning "people of the stinking water." This appellation was not intended to be an insult. It referred to the waters of the Fox River and Lake Winnebago, which were turbid and rich in algae at certain seasons of the year. The French translated it to "stinking people," which, for obvious reasons, made it a name the Ho-Chunk people never appreciated.

Hochungra, the name by which the Ho-Chunk described themselves, translates to "people of the big voice" or "people of the sacred language."[1] This refers to the Ho-Chunk belief that they represent the original people from whom all Siouan-speaking people sprang. The Ho-Chunk are most closely related to the Iowa, Oto, and Missouri tribes, which were part of the Ho-Chunk nation at one time. According to oral history, the four tribes split apart shortly before European contact.

Ho-Chunk are also related linguistically to the Osage, Quapaw, Omaha, Kansas, and Ponca peoples, as well as the Mandan in North Dakota and Siouan-speaking people in the southeastern United States. The fact that the Ho-Chunk are situated in the geographic center of all these people lends weight to the Hochungra contention that they are the "original people" and explains why the Iowa, Oto, and Missouri tribes refer to the Ho-Chunk even today as "grandfathers."

Although Ho-Chunk culture today is patrilineal, meaning descent and clan

Yellow Thunder
(second from right)
and a contingent of
Ho-Chunk in
Washington,
circa 1880.
WHi(X3)53938

membership derive from the father's side, some anthropologists believe that the Ho-Chunk originally were matrilineal. They speculate that this shift may have been the result of extensive intermarriage with neighboring patrilineal tribes in the seventeenth century and involvement in the fur trade, which emphasized male activities. Clans descend from two major divisions, or moieties: an earth division comprising eight clans, and a sky division with four clans. The earth division includes the Bear Clan, from which war chiefs were selected. The sky division includes the Thunderbird Clan, which traditionally produced the peace chiefs. Together, these leaders governed with the help of a council made up of principal members of each clan. They guided day-to-day activities in the large villages the Ho-Chunk inhabited at the time of European contact. Their closest neighbors were the Menominee, who were also their closest allies, and the Illinois, who were sworn enemies.

The Ho-Chunk believe they originated at Moga-Shooch (Red Banks), on the south shore of Green Bay, the deep notch between thumb and fingers on today's map of Wisconsin.[2] They were the most powerful tribe in the area, with homelands that extended from Upper Michigan to southern Wisconsin. Sometime during the century that preceded European contact, the Anishinabe (Ojibwe, Potawatomi, and Ottawa) began moving into the Ho-Chunk's territory along the shore of Lake Huron to the confluence of Lakes Michigan and Superior. The Anishinabe migration displaced the Menominee and the Ho-Chunk. One theory is that the loss of territory, combined with a growing population, created enough environmental stress that the Ho-Chunk began moving southward, which created antagonism with the tribes of the Illinois Confederacy (Kaskaskia, Peoria, and Illinois). With no place to expand, the Ho-Chunk split apart. Sometime around the year 1570, a tribal faction that would evolve into the Iowa, Oto, and Missouri left the main body of Ho-Chunk and headed west down the Wisconsin River to present-day Iowa, where they separated and evolved into three distinct tribes. The weakened main body of Ho-Chunk concentrated into large villages near Green Bay in order to defend their homeland against the encroaching Anishinabe from the north and the Illinois Confederacy from the south.

The population decline and economic dependence on European trade goods that accompanied Ho-Chunk participation in the fur trade left the tribe vulnerable to encroachment by white settlers, especially miners who were attracted to the rich lead deposits of the Upper Mississippi Valley. The indigenous people of the area had mined galena, the grayish lead ore, for at least eight thousand years. Women of the Sauk, Mesquakie, and Ho-Chunk nations worked the lead deposits every spring and fall, gathering enough of the mineral for personal use and sometimes collecting enough to trade with other Indians. The Ho-Chunk melted galena and used it as body paint, reserving the finest pieces for burial with their dead.

After the American Revolution (1775–1783), lead eclipsed fur as the principal means of exchange between the Ho-Chunk and white traders. In 1788, neighboring Sauk and Mesquakie formally leased a portion of their mineral lands to Julian Dubuque, a French miner who hired Native women, including Ho-Chunk, to work the mines. Soon this region, known as the Fever River Valley, was producing up to 40,000 pounds of lead bars, sheets, and bullets a year. As word spread of the richness of the deposits, the Ho-Chunk witnessed a steady stream of white miners pour into their territory "like wolves in the Plains to the dead buffalo," as Old Grayheaded Decora, a Ho-Chunk leader, described them. "They spread out in every direction and began to dig and find and carry off lead on the Winnebago lands."[3]

When the United States dramatically expanded its territory with the Louisiana Purchase (1803), the Ho-Chunk discovered that their homeland, once at the edge of American territory, was now in the middle of it. As war with Britain loomed, the Fever River Valley took on more importance as a strategic source of lead for ammunition. The federal government encouraged white encroachment by offering miners generous leases in exchange for ten percent royalties. Alarmed by the number of lead miners trespassing on their territory, the Ho-Chunk responded to the pan-Indian call to arms by Tecumseh, who was trying to repel white encroachment into the Ohio Valley. Enthusiastically endorsing the religious exhortations of Tecumseh's brother—Tenskwatawa, the Shawnee Prophet—the Ho-Chunk became one of the most militant members of Tecumseh's alliance. By 1809, the Ho-Chunk had established a permanent Hochungra village near Prophetstown (Tippecanoe) in present-day Indiana.

In 1811, Tenskwatawa disregarded his brother's orders not to provoke the Americans and, during Tecumseh's absence, attacked William Henry Harrison's troops. In what became known as the Battle of Tippecanoe, the Ho-Chunk and other members of the alliance suffered a tremendous defeat. The Ho-Chunk, furious, took Tenskwatawa prisoner for several weeks. It was only Tecumseh's return that saved Tenskwatawa from being killed. With assistance from the Ho-Chunk, Tecumseh was able to put his alliance back together. When the War of 1812 began, the united tribes threw their support to the British.[4]

The Ho-Chunk played a prominent role in war. Along with the Sauk, Mesquakie, and Potawatomi, they besieged Fort Madison in Illinois and forced the Americans to abandon it. They also fought at the battles of Maumee in Ohio and the River Raisin in Michigan. Even after Tecumseh was killed in battle in Ontario in October 1813, the Ho-Chunk continued to help the British repel an American attack at Fort Michilimackinac.

Following the Treaty of Ghent (1814), which ended the War of 1812, a portion of the Ho-Chunk signed a peace treaty with the Americans in St. Louis. The pact did not include land cessions, although some Ho-Chunk correctly feared that a land grab was inevitable, and many remained hostile to the American intruders in their homelands and even charged them a toll to travel through their country.

By 1825, more than ten thousand miners had illegally invaded the area. Hoping that an agreement with the federal government would firmly establish their boundaries, the Ho-Chunk and numerous other tribes signed the "Peace and Friendship Treaty" at Prairie du Chien.[5] However, two years later nothing had changed. "There are a great many Americans on our land, working it without permission," Four Legs, a Ho-Chunk chief, told a council at Butte des Morts. "And I want you to tell our Great Father to stop it, to reach out his long arm and draw them back."[6]

Ho-Chunk anxiety heightened in June 1827 with rumors that several of the tribe's warriors had been executed at Fort Snelling in the Minnesota Territory. Red Bird, a Ho-Chunk war chief, retaliated by attacking the home of white squatters south of La Crosse and killing several family members. Later, he attacked a barge carrying miners and mining supplies near Prairie du Chien. For three months, the Ho-Chunk resisted pressure to turn over Red Bird to white authorities, but eventually they prevailed on Red Bird to surrender. In September 1827, he gave himself up to Major William Whistler, pleading to be executed then and there. "I am ready," he told Whistler. "I do not wish to be put in irons. Let me be free. I have given away my life."[7] Despite his pleas, Red Bird was shackled and sentenced to hang at a later date.

Red Bird surrenders to Major William Whistler in Portage, September 1827.
Painting by Hugo Ballin; WHi(X3)21894

Red Bird's resistance had made him a hero to many Ho-Chunk, and his honorable surrender had even earned the grudging respect of many white officials. Still, it came as a surprise to many that a Ho-Chunk delegation to Washington was able to obtain a release and a presidential pardon for Red Bird. Unfortunately, it was too late. In February 1828, the war chief died of dysentery while imprisoned in Prairie du Chien.

The Ho-Chunk mission to Washington and Red Bird's ill-fated pardon proved costly to the tribe. In order to secure his release, the Ho-Chunk had agreed to give up their lead-rich lands in Illinois. A year later, they learned that U.S. officials wanted all their mineral lands south of the Wisconsin River. "Do you want *our* Country? Yours is much larger than ours," said the Ho-Chunk speaker Little Elk to the government's negotiators. "Do you want *our* wigwams? You live in palaces. My fathers, what can be your motive?"

The Ho-Chunk problems intensified in 1829 when national attention turned to a neighboring Sauk war chief whose lands near present-day Rock Island, Illinois, had been ceded in a fraudulent treaty twenty-five years earlier. When U.S. officials informed Black Hawk that he must abandon his village, he initially refused. Eventually he agreed to move to the Iowa side of the Mississippi River, only after officials promised to replace the corn his people had planted. When the corn arrived, the Sauk discovered it to be inferior both in quality and quantity. Later, Black Hawk remembered that his band was forced to sneak over in the night "to steal corn from their own fields . . . where they were discovered by the whites and fired upon."[8]

In 1832, Black Hawk's band sought refuge in Illinois with White Cloud, a Ho-Chunk prophet of Sauk and Ho-Chunk ancestry, who invited them to plant their corn in his village. As Black Hawk crossed the Mississippi and led his people northeastward toward White Cloud's village, regular army troops and several ragtag militias moved to intercept him. Lacking widespread support from the Ho-Chunk and disappointed that help from the British did not materialize, Black Hawk attempted several times, unsuccessfully, to surrender. For sixteen weeks, his warriors created diversions while the main body of Sauk—exhausted, starving, reduced to eating tree bark—fled from the militia. Eventually Black Hawk's retreat ended in the so-called Battle of Bad Axe (August 1832), which was little more than a massacre of Sauk men, women, and children as they attempted to cross the Mississippi south of La Crosse. Black Hawk's band, once numbering 1,200, had been reduced to 150 people.

The Black Hawk War divided the Ho-Chunk. Some enthusiastically supported the Sauk war chief. Most remained neutral. Others,

Black Hawk (1767–1838), Sauk warrior. Black Hawk's refusal to relocate his band to Iowa touched off the Black Hawk War in 1832. The U.S. Army and militias pursued Black Hawk's band throughout southwestern Wisconsin and massacred them near the Mississippi at the mouth of the Bad Axe River.
From *History of the Indian Tribes of North America* by McKenney and Hall, 1848; WHi(X3)38424

who had been terrorized by the Sauk, joined the Americans. White Crow, for example, agreed to fight against Black Hawk only after a coercive meeting with
Henry Dodge, a Missouri miner and slaveowner who arrived in 1828. Dodge, who
commanded a militia of lead miners and later would become Wisconsin's first
territorial governor, threatened that if the Ho-Chunk allowed Black Hawk to
camp with them, it would be interpreted as an act of war. In the summer of 1832,
he told a delegation of Ho-Chunk chiefs: "You will have your country taken from
you, your annuity money will be forfeited, and the lives of your people lost."[9]

Following the Black Hawk War, the Ho-Chunk were forced to cede their
lands south of the Wisconsin and Fox Rivers to the Rock River, encompassing
their cornfields, hunting grounds, and other significant sites, including De Jope
(Madison) and Neesh (Wisconsin Dells) in exchange for lands in western Iowa.
Five years later, twenty individual Ho-Chunk ceded the tribe's remaining lands
east of the Mississippi River and agreed to move to lands set aside for them in
Iowa. Tribal leaders protested in vain that of the signers, only two were from the
Bear Clan—the only clan authorized to conduct land negotiations.[10]

The 1820s signaled the beginning of the removal period for the Ho-Chunk. In
1837, the Americans offered the Ho-Chunk land they described as more desirable
than the Iowa tract and told them they had eight years to prepare for their move.
(It was only after the tribe received a written copy of the agreement that it
learned that the treaty actually read eight *months*.) The new land was in present-
day northern Minnesota near Long Prairie. In the view of U.S. negotiators, the
Ho-Chunk were to act as a buffer between enemy factions of Dakota and Ojibwe
—an unfortunate role for the displaced tribe, to say the least. Tribal leaders pressured federal officials for new lands.

Some Ho-Chunk, however, refused to leave their homelands, and others traveled to Iowa and Minnesota and returned. The Wisconsin Ho-Chunk today are
the descendants of the "renegades" or "rebel faction," as twenty-first-century tribal member Lance Tallmadge describes them, "who refused to move out west as
the reservations were established for them."[11]

In 1855, the Ho-Chunk in Long Prairie exchanged their lands for a reservation near Blue Earth, in south-central Minnesota. The reservation was not very
large, but the land was fertile and the Ho-Chunk farmed successfully. Life was
improving when the Civil War broke out in 1861. Many Ho-Chunk enlisted in the
Union Army, joining regiments from Minnesota, Nebraska, and Wisconsin.
While they were away, the Sioux Uprising (1862) claimed the lives of nearly five
hundred settlers. Although the Ho-Chunk were not part of the revolt, terrified
whites demanded that the Ho-Chunk be removed from the area along with the
Sioux. As a result, the government forced the Ho-Chunk to cede their lands at

Three Ho-Chunk women pose with their babies near Tomah, circa 1910. This photograph, like many others depicting Native Americans in their tribal dress, became a postcard.
Photo by A. C. Stone; WHi(X3)32712

Blue Earth for lands on the Crow Creek in South Dakota. The Ho-Chunk chief Baptiste visited the proposed site and bluntly reported: "It is damn cold country . . . no wood . . . damn bad country for Indians."[12]

In the winter of 1863, the government ordered the Ho-Chunk to move, ignoring Baptiste's objections and his pleas to wait for better weather. The chief's worst fears were realized when a quarter of the tribe—more than 550 of the nearly 2,000 tribal members—died en route to South Dakota. Many Ho-Chunk became ill from the rancid pork and rotten vegetables the government provided to the émigrés. Despite all this hardship and despair, however, the Ho-Chunk continued to resist removal. Of the 1,382 survivors, more than 1,200 fled in canoes down the Missouri River and took refuge among the Omaha in Nebraska. In 1865, the so-called treaty-abiding Ho-Chunk signed a treaty in which they purchased a portion of the Omaha reservation. There they remain to this day, a tribe politically distinct from the Ho-Chunk of Wisconsin.

Ho-Chunk tribal members in Wisconsin Dells, circa 1915. Postcards produced as early as 1890 suggest that the Ho-Chunk took an active role in Dells tourism.
WHS Archives, CF 94

The "renegades," the tough survivors who hid out in Wisconsin or returned from reservations in the west, were rounded up again and again and on one occasion were put into boxcars and shipped to Nebraska. Again, they made their way home. In 1874, as a little girl, Mountain Wolf Woman heard her mother's account of the last of the government's forced removal of the Wisconsin Ho-Chunk. There was "much rejoicing" at the train station when her family reunited with Nebraska relatives. However, by spring their joy had turned to fear when "great numbers" of Ho-Chunk began to die. She recalled in an interview in 1958 how her mother was frightened and disoriented by the tribe's removal to Nebraska: "Why do we stay here? I am afraid because the people are all dying. Why do we not go back home?"[13]

Within a year of their removal in 1874, about 650 of the 1,000 Wisconsin Ho-Chunk sent to Nebraska, including Mountain Wolf Woman's family, had gone home. Some who returned found leadership under Chiefs Dandy and Yellow Thunder, who had managed to secure a homestead in Wisconsin. Other Ho-Chunk followed suit, and in 1881 Congress passed special legislation allowing the Wisconsin Ho-Chunk forty-acre homesteads. Although the lands were inferior, most Ho-Chunk eked out an existence hunting, gathering, fishing, and gardening

Yellow Thunder, Ho-Chunk Chief, circa 1880. Yellow Thunder is believed to be the first Ho-Chunk who took up a homestead in western Wisconsin.

Courtesy of Jolley's, Portage City, Wisconsin; WHi(X3)11633

and occasionally hiring themselves out as farm hands.

By the turn of the century, the Ho-Chunk had also moved into the commercial cranberry market. Where once tribal members had gathered cranberries extensively for trade and personal use, now fences and private property signs marked their ancestral fields as belonging to white growers. Many Ho-Chunk went to work in the cranberry industry, only to be classified as migrant farm workers by the federal government. This was another stroke of bad luck for the Ho-Chunk. During the Great Depression of the 1930s, after government reformers instituted social security, Ho-Chunk elders who had worked for decades in the fields were ineligible for retirement benefits because their employers had not withheld social security payments from their paychecks.[14]

Tourism also played an important role in the lives of Ho-Chunk members, especially in the area known today as the Wisconsin Dells. In the early 1900s, tourists and vacationers who had seen and heard of the unsurpassed natural beauty of the river and its sandstone outcroppings began to arrive by train from Chicago, Milwaukee, the Twin Cities, and elsewhere. The Ho-Chunk were hired to entertain the tourists with traditional songs and dances at the Stand Rock Ceremonial and sold souvenirs—wood carvings, picture postcards, and distinctive baskets woven of black ash.

Ho-Chunk tribal members in Black River Falls in Jackson County, circa 1900.

Photo by Charles Van Schaick; WHi(V2)101

Mountain Wolf Woman, as an elder in the 1950s when she related the story of the Ho-Chunk Removal to anthropologist Nancy Oestreich Lurie.

Courtesy of the Speltz Studio, Black River Falls, Wisconsin

Like other Indians in Wisconsin, the Ho-Chunk faced intense pressure to assimilate. Christianity had been introduced as early as 1670 when French Jesuit Claude Allouez established a mission at the mouth of the Oconto River. Other Catholic missions followed in Prairie du Chien and Polonia in Portage County. In 1878, the Evangelical Reformed Church began a mission school near Black River Falls. Six years later, Norwegian Lutherans established a mission and boarding school a few miles from Wittenberg in Shawano County. Tension between these contending Protestants and Catholics eventually led to a reorganization of the Indian boarding school program. The government phased out subsidies to sectarian schools and opened more of its own boarding schools, including the Tomah Indian Industrial School. Present-day Ho-Chunk literature suggests that economic interests also played a part in this missionary fervor: "The missionaries vied with each other for souls, and for Indian school contracts."[15]

A government school opened at Tomah in January 1893 with seven employees and six students, all of them Ho-Chunk. Until 1934, when it closed, the Tomah School provided both an academic curriculum and manual training, along with music, athletics, religious instruction, and military training. By 1901, it had grown to two dozen teachers and 173 students—twenty-three over capacity. Of all the government boarding schools in Wisconsin, Tomah had per-

Ho-Chunk women in Van Schaick's portrait gallery, Black River Falls, circa 1915.
Photo by Charles Van Schaick; WHi(V2)729

haps the best reputation. Its superintendent, Ludley M. Compton, was a member of the Indian Rights Association and made a practice of hiring Indian staff, including teachers. But despite the relatively tolerant culture Compton established, school officials discouraged Ho-Chunk children from speaking their Native language and expressing their traditional culture. Often children as young as six were placed in the Tomah School and prevented from returning home until after they graduated from high school. Inevitably the experience resulted in family and community disassociation. A century later, many Ho-Chunk still wonder: Was the education worth the price?[16]

In 1934, when tribes were offered under the Indian Reorganization Act (IRA) the opportunity to create constitutional governments, the Ho-Chunk declined. An effort in the U.S. Court of Claims in 1928 to obtain redress for past wrongs had failed, and many Ho-Chunk were unwilling to accept IRA funds until their claim against the United States was settled. In 1946, tribal members elected a committee to bring suit with the Nebraska Winnebago under the Indian Claims Commission Act. This panel evolved into the Acting Wisconsin Winnebago Business Committee, which focused on meeting the health, education, housing, and welfare needs of tribal members. There was some question whether a nonreservation tribe such as the Ho-Chunk was even eligible for the IRA benefits of a constitutional government. However, a sympathetic official in the administration of President John F. Kennedy found an obscure Ho-Chunk homestead that had

Above: In 1993, the Ho-Chunk joined the InterTribal Bison Cooperative with four head of bison. By Autumn 2001 the tribe counted nearly 150 bison in its herd. The buffalo roam on 639 acres of restored prairie along the lower Wisconsin River near Muscoda.
Photo courtesy of Ho-Chunk Nation

Left: Harry Whitehorse, Ho-Chunk master carver and sculptor.
Photo by Skot Weidemann Photography, courtesy of Whitehorse Gallery

been declared tribal trust land. "We formed [as a tribe] under forty acres of land that was underwater—almost swampland," recalled WBBC member Richard Day. "That's all the tribe had—forty acres that nobody owned, but the tribe did."[17]

With the encouragement of most Ho-Chunk and the assistance of Indian advocacy groups such as the National Congress of American Indians, the committee began work on a Ho-Chunk constitution. In a referendum conducted in January 1963, Ho-Chunk from as far away as California overwhelmingly ratified the document. The tribal land base expanded in the 1960s when the Evangelical Reformed Church (now United Church of Christ) gave the Ho-Chunk its original church and mission property in Black River Falls. These 150 acres became the core of tribal trust land.

Then in 1974, the Ho-Chunk won a $4.6 million judgment from the Indian Claims Commission to compensate the tribe for its lands lost through fraudulent treaties. For elders, such as Bernadine Tallmadge, this compensation was too little and the resolution too dear: "Four point six million dollars, and you divide that

Ho-Chunk drummer
Paul Smith at Red Cloud
Park in Jackson County.
Photo by John Froelich;
WHi(X3)20504

among the Winnebago population. What did we get?" she asked. "We just sold our birthright."[18]

Today the 5,800 members of the Ho-Chunk Nation hold title to more than two thousand acres of land scattered across twelve northern Wisconsin counties. Despite the difficulties of providing service to a far-flung population, the Nation operates scores of tribal programs, including health clinics, Head Start centers, and economic development activities in each of its communities. Much of the tribe's economic successes have been fueled by profits from its four gaming operations—Lake Delton, Nekoosa, Black River Falls, and Madison. These, in turn, have allowed the Ho-Chunk to expand their enterprises to include hotels, restaurants, convenience stores, and gas stations, all of which contribute significantly to the local and state economies.

In 1993, the Ho-Chunk reintroduced a small herd of bison to tribal trust lands along the Wisconsin River near Muscoda. Two years later, they received a gift of twenty-five surplus animals from Badlands National Park. Today, with support from the InterTribal Bison Cooperative, a network of Indian Nations working to restore the buffalo, the Ho-Chunk maintain a herd of nearly 150 animals and hope to expand their bison herd to 400.[19]

Many Ho-Chunk members believe the greatest challenge facing the tribe remains their lack of a land base. In 1998, the Ho-Chunk applied to the General Services Administration for part ownership of the "mothballed" Badger Army Ammunition Plant, one of the most contaminated sites in Wisconsin, near Baraboo. The Ho-Chunk hope the federal government will agree to return 3,050 acres of land around the site, which the tribe has pledged to restore to prairie and use for bison habitat. For the "People of the Big Voice," this petition offers an opportunity to establish a sizeable Ho-Chunk reservation—and thus to continue and expand the tribe's legacy as a political and cultural force in Wisconsin.[20]

⑤ Ojibwe

The Anishinabe remember a time when they lived "on the shore of the Great Salt Water in the East." In the words of Ojibwe medicine man Edward Benton-Banai, their numbers were so great, "if one was to climb the highest mountain and look in all directions, they would not be able to see the end of the nation."[1] This eastern domain, however, had not always been their home. According to oral tradition, their original homes were in the Great Lakes region, where long ago the Creator, Gichi-Manidoo, had placed them on the last of the Four Worlds he created. He taught them everything they needed to know and gave them medicines to keep them healthy.

Over time, however, the people lost their way and began to quarrel among themselves, so Gichi-Manidoo told them to leave. They migrated east and were gone so long they forgot the way home. Sometime later, speaking through a prophet, Gichi-Manidoo told them it was time to return. They were to follow a Sacred Shell that would lead them to seven stopping places and, ultimately, to the "Food that Grows on Water."

Perhaps as early as 1500 B.P., the Anishinabe, an alliance that includes the Ojibwe, Potawatomi, and Ottawa, left their homes along the Atlantic Seaboard and traveled west. Among the stopping places were Kichi-ka-be-kong—a powerful place of "water and thunder" known today as Niagara Falls—and Baw-wa-ting, an excellent fishing area, which the French later renamed Sault Ste. Marie. The Anishinabe continued on to the site of present-day Duluth to a place known as "Spirit Island" and explored the south shore of Lake Superior. There, according to oral tradition, they found Manoomin, meaning wild rice, the "Food that Grows on Water." They also found their final resting stop: an island they called Mo-ning-wun-a-kawn-ing, translated as either "the place that was dug" or "the place of the gold-breasted woodpecker." In 1792, the eldest daughter of White Crane, the hereditary chief of the Crane Clan, married French fur trader Michel Cadotte and took the Christian name Madeleine. The Ojibwe renamed the island in her honor.

Logging on the Lac Courte Oreilles Ojibwe Reservation, 1909.
WHi(X3)37336

According to a copper plate belonging to Chief Tagwagane of the Crane Clan, the Ojibwe had arrived on Madeline Island well before Columbus encountered the New World. Tagwagane's ancestors had carved a notch with each passing generation. By 1844, nine indentations had been incised on the copper plate. Using a conservative life expectancy figure of forty years, approximately 360 years had passed since the Ojibwe had established a village on Madeline Island. According to this same medallion, the Ojibwe had encountered—or at least heard about—whites at least a decade before Jean Nicolet arrived in present-day Green Bay in 1634. Near the third notch, someone from that generation had etched the figure of a man in a large hat. The figure may have been Étienne Brûlé, who is believed to have explored Lake Superior in 1622.[2]

The Ojibwe enthusiastically embraced the French people who arrived after Brûlé and Nicolet. These European traders brought the Ojibwe marvelous new items: metal axes, iron cooking kettles, bright-colored cloth, and glass beads. They also introduced them to guns, which not only enabled the Ojibwe to become better hunters but also gave them an advantage over their enemies, especially the Bwaan, as the Ojibwe referred to the Dakota, with whom they fought for control of the rice beds.

Life among the Ojibwe bands, then as now, was organized around the seasons. In early spring, in addition to spearing fish, the Ojibwe processed maple

continued on facing page

RED CLIFF

2001 population: 4,144

1854 Treaty: 7,321 acres

1978: 7,267 acres (5,122 tribally owned)

1999: 7,962 acres (6,181 tribally owned)

BAD RIVER

2001 population: 6,790

1854 Treaty: 124,332 acres

1978: 41,802 acres (8,235 tribally owned)

1999: 56,283 acres (20,166 tribally owned)

LAC DU FLAMBEAU

2001 population: 3,057

1854 Treaty: 70,000 acres

1978: 40,479 acres (25,152 tribally owned)

1999: 44,947 acres (30,507 tribally owned)

syrup. The sap began to run when the temperatures turned warm: still freezing at night, but forty or fifty degrees during the day. The Ojibwe tapped the trees and collected the liquid in buckets made of birch bark. They slow-boiled the sap over a hickory-bark fire until it turned to sugar, which was eaten alone, mixed into other foods, or stored for use throughout the year.

In summer, Ojibwe men fished intensively and hunted minimally, while the women gathered nuts, berries, and other foods and planted gardens in which they grew corn, beans, squash, and potatoes. In late summer, the Ojibwe gathered to prepare the wild rice beds. A few weeks before the harvest, Ojibwe families bound together bundles of rice stalks. Each distinctive bundling marked a section of the bed as belonging to a particular family. Although there was no formal system of private property, families returned to the same sections of rice beds year after year and reseeded their areas so they would have a crop the next year. Others respected the right of each family to harvest in a particular place.

It appears that Ojibwe women traditionally did most of the ricing, although in 1942 a Lac Courte Oreilles elder insisted that "in the old days" men were responsible for the harvest. After the rice ripened, the Ojibwe paddled their canoes to the rice beds. With one person poling or slowly paddling through the beds, the other, using two lightweight sticks, gently "knocked" the rice kernels from the bound stalks into the floor of the canoe. The Ojibwe then spread the rice on woven mats for a day or two to remove the moisture.

Before the introduction of iron and copper kettles, the Ojibwe either dried the rice on scaffolds over slow-burning fires or parched it on hot stones in fire pits. Men or boys in clean moccasins then undertook the strenuous task of "dancing" the rice—treading on it in clay-lined tramping pits—in order to loosen the chaff from the kernel. Finally, the Ojibwe placed the rice in shallow birch bark winnowing baskets to separate the broken husks from the kernels. Wild rice—technically not rice at all, but rather an aquatic grass—was used in soups, stews, pancakes, and jerky. Nutritionally, it was vital to the Ojibwe diet. Spiritually and culturally, it was the embodiment of their covenant with the Creator, who had led them to the Food that Grows on Water.[3]

During the wintertime, the Ojibwe hunted white-tailed deer and trapped for beaver, fisher, otter, and other fur-bearing animals. Pelts, maple syrup, processed rice, and crops from their gardens became principal trade items, binding the

Ojibwe to the *voyageurs*, who moved between Indian communities and brokered items between the tribes and the French.

The affection between the French and the Ojibwe was so unqualified that the Ojibwe assimilated the French into their communities and adopted them into their families. They encouraged intermarriage, even absorbing the children of these unions into the tribe's warrior clan, the Marten Clan. As animosities between the French and English crept farther west into the western Great Lakes region, the Ojibwe—bound by friendship and kinship—offered the French their military support. Throughout the seventeenth century the Ojibwe fought alongside their allies against the English and their confederates, the Five Nations, or Haudenosaunee.

Madeline Island, with its major trading post at La Pointe, was not only the economic headquarters of the Ojibwe nation but also its spiritual center. The "Three Fires," as the Anishinabe referred to their religious alliance, returned to the island at various times of the year to conduct Midewiwin, or Great Medicine Lodge ceremonies. The Midewiwin, through its songs, stories, and rituals, embodied the spiritual heritage of the Anishinabe and offered a code of conduct to keep them culturally rooted and physically and spiritually healthy.

Shortly after Nicolet's visit, Jesuit missionaries began visiting La Pointe, and in 1665 Father Claude Allouez established his Saint Esprit Mission there. According to oral history, the intense effort by these "Black Coats" to convert the Ojibwe to Christianity divided the people. Ojibwe converts were encouraged to reject the traditional teaching of the Midewiwin Lodge. Factions developed. Religious divisions and environmental pressures, caused by an expanding population, led various bands of Ojibwe to leave the island in search of fish, game, and wild rice. These were the ancestors of the distinct Ojibwe bands that exist in Wisconsin today.

As the fur trade depleted the fur-bearing animals along the south shore of Lake Superior, the Ojibwe began pushing farther inland in search of pelts. This brought them into increasing conflict with the Mesquakie and Dakota. With guns acquired from the French, the Ojibwe had a distinct advantage over these two tribes, who still relied primarily on war clubs and bows and arrows. Each winter, the Ojibwe traveled west to the St. Croix and Chippewa River valleys to hunt deer, moose, elk, and other fur-bearing animals in the game-rich forests. Each spring they returned to La Pointe for Midewiwin ceremonies.

The Ojibwe had an intense relationship with the Dakota, sometimes warring with them, sometimes coexisting peacefully. During periods of amity, Ojibwe men and women intermarried with the Dakota. Today their descendants, along the east and west banks of the Mississippi River, reflect the intermingling of cul-

LAC COURTE OREILLES

2001 population: 5,513 + 2,000 ancillary

1854 Treaty: 70,000 acres

1978: 30,529 acres (3,945 tribally owned)

1999: 47,944 acres (22,869 tribally owned)

ST. CROIX OJIBWE

2001 population: 2,000

1934 Land Grant: 1,700 acres

1978: 1,715 acres (1,200 tribally owned)

1999: 2,712 acres (2,712 tribally owned)

SOKAOGON (MOLE LAKE)

2001 population: 1,207

1934 Land Grant: 1,700 acres

1978: 1,700 acres (1,700 tribally owned)

1999: 1,731 acres (1,731 tribally owned)

View of the
1825 Treaty held at
Prairie du Chien,
September 1825.
Sketch by J. O. Lewis, from
Thomas L. McKenney,
*Sketches of a Tour to the
Lakes,* 1827; WHi(X3)2812

tures. Often, however, the two nations fought bitterly. Throughout the French and English fur trade periods, the Ojibwe and the Dakota viewed each other with suspicion. By the early nineteenth century, diplomacy between the two tribes had broken down to the point that attacks and reprisals were almost continuous. In 1825, the United States invited the Ojibwe, Dakota, and other Indian nations in what would become the state of Wisconsin to meet at Prairie du Chien, ostensibly to negotiate a treaty of "peace and friendship." In actuality, the federal government was interested in stabilizing the area for western expansion and acquiring land from the Ojibwe. However, before it could begin cession treaties, it first had to establish tribal boundaries. Ojibwe-Dakota enmity was a convenient pretext.

Treating with the Lake Superior Ojibwe was no easy task. Because of the autonomous nature of the bands, the Ojibwe did not have one principal chief with whom federal officials could negotiate. Unlike a European monarchy, each Ojibwe band had several leaders and headmen who "governed" by consent of the people rather than by authority. "I do not speak altogether of my own mind," the young St. Croix war chief Lone Man told the assembly at Prairie du Chien, "but listen to the words of the collected chiefs." The 1825 treaty itself is clear evidence of the decentralized nature of Ojibwe politics. No fewer than forty-one Ojibwe "chiefs" and headmen signed the document.[4]

Although it is not clear that the Ojibwe leaders who signed the treaty at Prairie du Chien in 1825 were aware of the government's motives at the time, within twelve years they began to understand the full implications of treating with the United States. In 1830, President Andrew Jackson signed the Indian Removal Act, by which the United States claimed to have the authority to move tribes east of the Mississippi River to lands set aside for them in the West. The Ojibwe nervously watched as dozens of tribes, including other Anishinabe—the Potawatomi—were forcibly removed from their homelands.

Federal negotiators used not-so-subtle means of coercing concessions from the Ojibwe. A year after the Prairie du Chien council, federal negotiators met the

The treaty meeting at Fond du Lac, 1826

Sketch by J. O. Lewis, from Thomas L. McKenney, *Sketches of a Tour to the Lakes,* 1827. WHi(X3)35395

Ojibwe at Fond du Lac. Before the talks began, soldiers, who drilled, paraded, and demonstrated their firepower for the Ojibwe, provided a clear message. "You have never seen your great father's arm [the military]," one commissioner told the Ojibwe, "only a bit, and a very little bit, of his little finger." In addition to their weak military position in comparison to the federal government, the Ojibwe understood how their decentralized political structure placed them at a disadvantage: "We are a distracted people," Naudin (The Wind) told Territorial Governor Henry Dodge, "and have no regular system of acting together."

In the treaties of 1837 and 1842, the Ojibwe were forced to concede vast acres of land—nearly two-thirds of present-day northern Wisconsin, a portion of central Minnesota, and much of Michigan's Upper Peninsula. Historian David Wrone estimated that the Ojibwe gave up 170 billion board feet of timber, 150 billion tons of iron ore, and 15,000 lakes, as well as rivers, ports and power sites.[5] In exchange, the Ojibwe received $22,000 in annuities and $67,000 in goods and services. In addition, the tribe negotiated $115,000 for their mixed-blood relatives and $145,000 for traders to whom the Ojibwe were heavily in debt.

Nineteenth-century petition from Ojibwe clan chiefs. The animal figures represent clan leaders, the thick line represents Lake Superior, and the four small ovals represent the rice beds. This petition indicates that the Ojibwe are of one mind and one heart and do not wish to be removed from their wild rice beds near Lake Superior.

Henry Rowe Schoolcraft, *Historical and Statistical Information Respecting the History of the Indian Tribes . . . ,* Vol. I, 1851

There is evidence the Ojibwe believed they were merely leasing the land, not selling it. In 1864, an Ojibwe delegation to Washington delivered its written version of the 1837 treaty negotiations, in which the Ojibwe insisted they had sold the timber rights, not the rights to the land itself: "From the usual height of cutting a tree down and upwards to top is what I sell you, I reserve the root of the tree." In the 1837 treaty minutes, Chief Ma-ghe-ga-bo declared: "Of all the country that we grant you we wish to hold on to a tree [maple] where we get our living, & to reserve the streams where we drink the waters that give us life."[6]

The Ojibwe negotiators were also concerned about protecting the interests of future generations. In both the 1837 and 1842 treaties, the Ojibwe clearly reserved the right to hunt, fish, and gather on the land they ceded the United States government. Article 5 of the 1837 treaty stated: "The privilege of hunting, fishing and gathering the wild rice, upon the lands, the rivers and the lakes included in the territory ceded, is guarantied [sic] to the Indians, during the pleasure of the President of the United States." Likewise Article II of the 1842 treaty states: "The Indians stipulate for the right of hunting on the ceded territory, with the other usual privileges of occupancy, until required to remove by the President of the United States. . . ." The Ojibwe had been promised they would not be removed as long as they did not "misbehave." As they were to learn a mere six years later, this was a hollow promise.

By 1848, rumors that the Ojibwe would be removed to Minnesota had reached tribal leaders. From La Pointe, Chief Buffalo sent out runners to see if there had been any transgressions—to ask if the Ojibwe had, in fact, committed any "depredations" and broken the terms of the treaty. No such infractions were reported.

On February 6, 1850, at the urging of Commissioner of Indian Affairs William Medill, President Zachary Taylor signed the dreaded removal order. Although government officials insisted that they could better protect the Ojibwe from "injurious contact" with whites by moving them to Minnesota Territory, there were other motivations. Western expansionists believed the peaceful Ojibwe could be used as a buffer between white settlers and the more unpredictable Sioux. Minnesotans eagerly eyed the patronage jobs that accompanied Indian agencies, along with Indian annuities that sustained a corrupt network of white politicians, traders, and businessmen.

In an effort to coerce the Ojibwe to move, federal officials ordered that the 1850 annuity payments, normally paid at La Pointe—the centrally located heart of the Ojibwe Nation—instead be made at Sandy Lake, Minnesota. More than four hundred Ojibwe traveled hundreds of miles to claim those annuities, only to die from starvation, disease, and exposure at Sandy Lake in the late fall and winter of 1850. "Our women and children do indeed cry, our Father, on account of their suffering from cold and hunger," Chief Buffalo dictated in an 1851 letter sent to the Commissioner of Indian Affairs. "We wish to . . . be permitted to remain here where we were promised we might live, as long as we were not in the way of the Whites."

For the next two years, Ojibwe chiefs and headmen begged Washington officials to reconsider the removal order. In spring 1852, Chief Buffalo, who was then ninety-three years old, traveled by foot, canoe, and railroad to Washington to plead his peoples' case. Buffalo managed to get an audience with President

Annuity payment to the Ojibwe at La Pointe on Madeline Island, circa 1852.
WHi(X3)12939

Millard Fillmore and persuaded him to smoke the peace pipe. He and Chief O-sho-ga explained that the Ojibwe had been told in both the 1837 and 1842 treaties that the government was not interested in the land, only the pine and the minerals. In their minds they had never ceded the land itself. Two days after the meeting, President Fillmore rescinded the removal order and began the process of setting up permanent reservations for the Ojibwe. Buffalo, O-sho-ga, and the four other members of their party returned by rail and steamship to St. Paul, Minnesota, and then went overland to Lake Superior. Along the way, they spread the news to various Ojibwe bands, which "caused great rejoicing."

In 1854, Ojibwe chiefs and headmen gathered for the last time for treaty talks with U.S. negotiators. Although there was excitement and relief, the Ojibwe were wary. Chief Na-gon-ab no doubt spoke for many when he told the commissioners that the Ojibwe felt that they were misled by the 1837 and 1842 treaties. "Does the great father tell the truth?" he asked. "Does he keep his promises?" Na-gon-ab, a noted orator and principal chief of the Fond du Lac band, told the assembly that the Ojibwe had committed the treaty to memory and had kept faithfully to it. Their memorized version differed from the written version—the "black marks"— as he put it:

You go to your black marks and say this is what those men put down; this is what they said when they made the treaty. The men we talk with don't come back; they do not come and you tell us they did not tell us so. We ask where they are? You say you do not know or that they are dead and gone.

To protect themselves, the Ojibwe asked Benjamin Armstrong, Buffalo's adopted son, to guard their interests during the 1854 negotiations. An Alabama native who had traveled north for health reasons in 1835, Armstrong spoke fluent Ojibwe and had served as Buffalo's interpreter at the historic meeting with Fillmore. Armstrong recommended several changes and advised the chiefs to delay the signing ceremony until they were made. Ojibwe leaders were insistent upon two provisions: first, that they establish reservations at "different points of the country that would suit their convenience," and second, that they retain the right to hunt, fish, and gather on the land they had agreed to give up.[7]

As a result of the negotiations, the Ojibwe created four reservations: Bad River (124,332 acres), Lac Courte Oreilles (70,000 acres), Lac du Flambeau (70,000 acres), and Red Cliff (7,321 acres). Of the millions of acres that represented the original Ojibwe homeland, after the 1854 treaty fewer than 275,000 acres remained. As they had in the earlier treaties, the Ojibwe in the 1854 negotiations insisted upon the right to hunt, fish, and gather in the land they had ceded: "And such of them as reside in the territory hereby ceded, shall have the right to hunt and fish therein, until otherwise ordered by the President." The wisdom of the Ojibwe leaders in reserving this right for future generations would become evident more than century later.

The signature page of the 1854 treaty reflects the shifting political identities of the Ojibwe bands and is significant not only for which names appear, but also for which names do not. Leaders of the St. Croix and Sokaogon (Mole Lake) Ojibwe apparently did not attend the negotiation sessions or, if they did, failed to sign the treaty. As a result, both tribes would remain landless for nearly eighty years before negotiating reservations of their own. By reducing the Ojibwe to just four reservations in Wisconsin, the federal government attempted to consolidate the Ojibwe and impose new generalized identities on tribal members. In this vision of containment, the residents of Yellow River, Mud Lake, and Old Post did not have distinct band identities but rather became simply Lac Courte Oreilles.

The size of the Bad River Reservation suggests that federal officials may have expected that the Ojibwe who were left out of the treaty, including the scattered bands along the St. Croix River, would attach themselves to the Ojibwe at Bad River. Although some of the distinctiveness that then marked each band has been lost to time, it is important to understand that differences did exist and sometimes shaped how the bands responded to historical challenges, especially in regard to their treaty rights.

The bands did share the pain of common experiences, such as forced assimilation through allotment and Indian boarding schools. In 1887, Congress passed the General Allotment Act by which reservation land was divided in severalty and allotted to individual tribal members in eighty-acre parcels. In actuality, limited allotment had already begun at Lac Courte Oreilles (1881) and Bad River (1883). To ensure that the new Native landowners would be exposed to the supposed "civilizing" effects of the Christian work ethic, Indian lands that remained after federal officials completed the allotment process were sold to whites. Although Indian land was supposed to be held in trust for twenty-five years, during which time Native people could not sell their allotments, the government made exemptions for Indians judged "competent"—meaning they could read and write English and make informed decisions about their property. During the trust period, a surprising number of Ojibwe became "competent" enough to lose their land. By the time allotment ended in 1934, the allotment policy had reduced the Ojibwe

FIRST PEACE COUNCIL EVER HELD BETWEEN CHIPPEWAS SIOUXS, "BUFFALO BILL" PEACE MAKER.

William "Buffalo Bill" Cody in Ashland in 1896, during negotiations for the "Peace Treaty" he helped arrange between the Ojibwe and the Sioux.

WHi(X3)1985

land base in Wisconsin from 271,653 to 160,561 acres—a loss of more than forty percent.

The boarding school experience did to Ojibwe culture what the General Allotment Act had done to Ojibwe land. As early as 1856, Ojibwe children were taken from their homes and placed in government boarding schools, where school officials discouraged them from speaking their language or practicing their traditional religions and customs. Through much of the late nineteenth and early twentieth centuries, Ojibwe parents had no say in which schools their children would attend. Most Ojibwe children went to one of three government-run schools, in Hayward, Tomah, or Lac du Flambeau. Some went to parochial schools, such as St. Mary's School, run by the Franciscan Sisters of Perpetual Adoration on the Bad River Reservation. Other children were sent as far away as the Carlisle Indian School in Pennsylvania, where they received instruction in a quasimilitary atmosphere. Most of the schools in Wisconsin patterned them-

One of the many
prolific Ojibwe
beadwork artists.
WHi(X3)12224

selves after the Carlisle model, providing a half-day of academic instruction and a half-day of manual training. As one critic complained in 1914, "When an Indian is 14 years of age and enters a white school, he is practically only as far advanced as a child who would be in knickerbockers."

To be sure, some Ojibwe were able to rise above the mediocrity of Indian boarding schools and enter professional fields. The vast majority, however, became part of a growing underclass of young Indian adults with marginal skills. Indian men became hired farm hands or laborers. Indian women entered domestic service. A formal system of exploitation, known as the "outing system," solidified this marginalization. Instead of returning to their homes during summer vacation, boarding school students worked for exploitive wages in white homes. "For the present I will pay her $1.25 per week as I consider that this is all she is worth to me," said Mrs. J. T. Martin of Lucy, an eighteen-year-old Ojibwe girl from the Lac du Flambeau School. "I think the Indian girls naturally slow and this of course is a hard fault to overcome." For that dollar and a quarter—less than half the wage paid to white midwestern domestics—Lucy was expected to work twelve hours a day, six days a week.[8]

Throughout the difficult years of forced assimilation, the Ojibwe struggled not only to construct their identities as new Americans, but also to maintain their identities as Native Americans and members of their distinct bands. It is a remarkable achievement and a tribute to the persistence of culture that six Ojibwe communities survived the intense pressure on their lands and traditional teachings to maintain their tribal identity in Wisconsin.

Lac Courte Oreilles

In about 1745, three brothers of the Bear Clan led their families to Odaawaazaaga'igan, an abandoned Ottawa camp on the east shore of Lac Courte Oreilles near present-day Hayward, and established a permanent village. There are two versions of the story. In one, the clan traveled to the large lake where they found the frozen body of an Ottawa Indian. Believing this to be a powerful sign, they pitched their lodges not far from the spot and established their village. In the other, more accepted version, a young member of the clan died during the winter. Unable to bury the child because of the hardness of the ground, the grieving family stayed with the body to protect it from wolves and scavengers. Spring turned to summer, and the clan decided to make the area its permanent home. Additional Ojibwe families gravitated to the area, settled on the west fork of the Chippewa River, and named their settlement *Pahquahwong*, meaning "where the river is wide." To the French, however, *Pahquahwong* was known as *Lac Courte Oreilles*—"Lake of the Short Ears." This referred to the earlier Ottawa inhabitants, who, unlike the Ojibwe, did not wear heavy earrings that stretched their ear lobes. From Lac Courte Oreilles, the Ojibwe pushed farther west to the Mississippi River and established other Ojibwe settlements along the St. Croix River.

Before the 1854 treaty, which established the Lac Courte Oreilles Reservation, Chief Aw-ke-wain-ze (The Old Man) was said to have walked the perimeter of the lands he had chosen for his people's reservation, taking great care to choose those that contained the most productive rice beds. The band's precious resource, however, soon fell victim to competing interests: logging, flood control, and the desire for hydroelectric power.

Soon after the Ojibwe land cessions, timber companies began cutting down the pine forests near the Lac Courte Oreilles Reservation. After allotment, the Bureau of Indian Affairs granted contracts to lumber companies to cut timber on the reservation itself. Since it was cheaper to float the logs rather than transporting them overland to sawmills downstream, lumber companies and even some Ojibwe constructed dams to control the water flow along the Chippewa River and its tributaries.

The need for flood control and hydroelectric power grew with the lumber towns and farming communities that sprang up along the Chippewa River down-

Indian veterans return to the Lac Courte Oreilles Reservation following World War I. The Ojibwe joined 25,000 Native soldiers who volunteered for service even though they were not citizens.
Photo by Charles Brown; WHi(X3)18963

river from the Lac Courte Oreilles. Beginning in 1912, the Wisconsin-Minnesota Light & Power Company (W-MLP) began acquiring the permits and property necessary to build a massive dam that would flood 5,600 acres of reservation land, inundating maple groves, cranberry bogs, wild rice beds, cemeteries, and the village of Pahquahwong itself.

The company promised to move Indian graves to an upland site and build a new village on higher ground. It also promised to replant the rice beds and compensate the Ojibwe for the loss of their annual harvest. The Lac Courte Oreilles vehemently objected. Over the next decade, tribal leaders used every legal and administrative means possible to block the dam. On August 8, 1921, however, the Federal Power Commission, over the objections of the tribe, granted a fifty-year license to build and operate the dam.

Two years later, the floodgates closed and reservation lands began to fill with water. By late summer of 1923, twenty-five feet of water covered the village of Pahquahwong and the resources that had sustained it for nearly two centuries. The company had broken its promises. When the remains of hundreds of deceased Ojibwe began washing ashore, a horrified community learned that

Children at the drum during the Winter Dam Protest at Lac Courte Oreilles, 1971. LCO members, aided by members of the American Indian Movement, took over the dam to protest a lease extension for Northern States Power Company. The occupation ended with NSP granting concessions to the LCO tribe.
WHi(X3)46262

seven hundred Indian graves were left behind. Further, the water level in the newly created impoundment fluctuated dramatically, making it impossible to sustain new rice beds. The Ojibwe learned a sad truth about the reservoir that became known as the Chippewa Flowage: "The Food that Grows on Water" could not grow on this water.[9]

Lac du Flambeau

Sometime before 1745, Sha-da-wish, a chief of the Crane Clan, led his extended family to the headwaters of the Wisconsin River, near Lac Vieux Desert. After the Ojibwe pushed the Mesquakie Indians west, Sha-da-wish's son, Keesh-ke-mun (Sharpened Stone), continued his father's mission. In their lightweight birch bark canoes, Keesh-ke-mun's band followed the river south, paddling and portaging to the maze of interlocking lakes and streams near present-day Minocqua. They established their village where the Bear River exits Flambeau Lake.

Oral tradition tells of a nearly blind old man who taught the Ojibwe how to "fire hunt" for fish. At night, by the light of pitch-filled birch bark torches, the Ojibwe speared pike, suckers, and muskellunge, which became an important part of their diet. The Ojibwe called the fire hunters *Waswaagan,* and the community

Girls at the Lac du Flambeau Boarding School, circa 1890.
WHi(X3)35355

became known among the other bands as *Was-waagaming*. French fur traders, who witnessed the spearing ritual, called the village *Lac du Flambeau,* meaning "Lake of the Torches."

Lac du Flambeau remained an important center for trade, first for the French and then for the British, who established a year-round outpost on Flambeau Lake in 1792. After the War of 1812, the American Fur Company moved in and continued to maintain a presence at Lac du Flambeau until 1842. After the 1854 treaty, federal officials surveyed the land and set aside three townships for the reservation, adding a fourth in 1866. The next twenty years brought railroad and stagecoach service. Soon, loggers, settlers, and entrepreneurs pushed into the region, drawn by its rich forests and myriad clear lakes.

By 1894, the Flambeau Lumber Company was cutting 30 million board feet of white pine timber annually on the reservation. In letters to Washington, tribal leaders continually complained that the company capriciously cut timber that did not belong to them and did not always honor the lumber contracts they had signed with tribal members. Furthermore, their Indian agent controlled their allotment money and allowed them just ten dollars a month in the form of a coupon redeemable only at Flambeau Lumber's "company store." The store itself, and the system it represented, created hardships for the tribe. At a U.S. Senate hearing in 1909, Charles Headflyer, a Lac du Flambeau shopowner, told investigators that he sold flour for "ten cents cheaper than they were selling it at the company store" yet still could not compete. "I have a little store, trying to make a living, and all I got in the way of orders is $5 this whole summer."[10]

Much of the tribe's attention at the turn of the century was focused on the government boarding school, which was built in 1895 and was notorious for its heavy-handedness toward Indian children. Albert Cobe, who attended the school, recalled a small jail located behind the school near the road. Cobe remembered a mustached disciplinarian beating him with a length of garden hose after he tried to run away. A friend of his, who also tried to escape, was taken to the basement and ordered to crawl about on his hands and knees. Apparently, the mustached man forgot about the boy. "When morning came, we all filed down-stairs for the shower, and found him on the floor, crying," Cobe remembered. "His hands and knees were all bloody."

The first few decades of the twentieth century were difficult ones for the Lac du Flambeau. Twin assaults on Ojibwe land and culture had weakened the band. When tourism replaced timber as the area's leading industry, some Ojibwe men found employment as hunting and fishing guides. Lac du Flambeau women earned income selling beadwork, weavings, and baskets to appreciative visitors. However, most tribal members found it difficult to eke out a living. By a variety of means—foreclosures, skullduggery, and their own naivete—the Lac du Flambeau had lost much of their land base. White vacationers and resort owners now owned most of the tribe's prime waterfront property. More and more, the Lac du Flambeau found themselves outsiders on their own reservation.[11]

Red Cliff

Ojibwe who remained in the vicinity of Madeline Island after the Ojibwe diaspora in the mid-eighteenth century became known collectively as the La Pointe Band, named after the primary village on the island. Although most La Pointe Ojibwe did not permanently reside on the island, Madeline remained the "center of the earth" for them. The La Pointe Ojibwe actually represented more than a dozen bands that lived along Lake Superior's south shore and traveled back and forth to trade and to attend Midewiwin cere-monies.

Missionary activity among the Ojib-we, especially by Roman Catholic priests, intensified during the early nineteenth century. Some chiefs, including Buffalo, converted to Christianity. However, a ma-jority of Ojibwe chiefs and headmen con-tinued to follow the old ways. The 1854 treaty allowed the two factions to solidify

Chief Buffalo, Principal Chief of the Ojibwe. In 1852, Buffalo traveled to Washington, D.C., and persuaded President Millard Fillmore to rescind an earlier order removing the Ojibwe to Sandy Lake, Minnesota. Buffalo was instrumental in securing four of the six Ojibwe reservations in Wisconsin.
WHi(X3)41266

Frank Montano, Red Cliff
Ojibwe flute maker and
musician.
Photo courtesy of Frank
Montano

a division that had been evolving for decades. The Christianized Ojibwe, under the leadership of Chief Buffalo, took up permanent residence near the red cliffs of Buffalo Bay near the tribe's traditional fishing grounds. The other group established themselves at Bad River, where the Ojibwe had planted gardens every year. Despite this physical separation, the two groups maintained cordial relations.

Buffalo's band settled on the 7,321 acres their chief had negotiated under terms of the 1854 treaty. The community relied heavily on fishing. Ojibwe women fashioned large gill nets from basswood, nettle, and other natural fibers. Men carved cedar floats and stone sinkers. Ojibwe fishermen, in birch bark canoes, set their nets on deepwater reefs far offshore. As early as 1830, tribal fishermen were providing the American Fur Company with lake trout and whitefish on a commercial basis. By 1837, the enterprise was producing more than two thousand barrels of fish a year.

With their small boats and handmade nets, the Red Cliff Ojibwe found it difficult to compete with the large commercial fleets who were attracted to the rich fishing waters of Superior's south shore. By the 1880s, the tribe's small fishing operation had fallen on hard times, and more and more tribal members worked for non-Indian fishing interests in nearby Bayfield.

In 1873, tribal logging began on the Red Cliff Reservation. After the Commissioner of Indian Affairs approved construction of a sawmill, members of the Red Cliff Band began cutting timber for frame houses. In 1896, the Indian agent awarded a contract to the Red Cliff Lumbering Company, which harvested nine million board feet of white and Norway pine, hemlock, and spruce the following year. Many Red Cliff tribal members found employment as loggers, scalers, and millworkers. Within a decade, however, nearly all the timber was gone. Poor logging practices had left many thousands of acres littered with slash piles that were vulnerable to fire. The prohibitive cost of stump removal made the ravaged landscape expensive to clear and difficult to farm.

When the mill burned down in 1906, it was never rebuilt. Red Cliff Ojibwe found themselves on the downside of timber's boom-and-bust cycle. Some tribal members went to work for mining companies, mostly as woodchoppers and loaders. Others loaded and unloaded freighters for Great Lakes shipping companies.

A few returned to fishing. Others supported themselves by working in non-Indian shops and factories or by hiring themselves out as farmhands.

By 1929, few Red Cliff Ojibwe even felt the effects of the Great Depression. Their economy had already been depressed for years. Ninety-five percent of tribal members had sold or lost their lands to foreclosures.[12]

Bad River

When the so-called "pagan" La Pointe chiefs chose their 120,000-acre reservation site under terms of the 1854 treaty, they selected an area that contained 16,000 acres of high-quality wetlands, including the rich rice-producing Kakagon and Bad River Sloughs along Lake Superior's south shore. This was the area that had sustained the Ojibwe for generations. They called their settlement simply *Odanah*—the Ojibwe word for "village."

The attempt to separate themselves from their Christian relatives was not successful. In 1856, federal officials agreed to pay the American Board of Commissioners for Foreign Missions, which had established an ecumenical mission at Odanah some years earlier, $900 to educate eight boys and eleven girls. In a letter to the board, J. M. Gordon wrote: "An Indian needs to be taught subjection to authority, love of labor, and systematic industry in some useful employment to make a civilised man of him. Without these elements of character, mere book knowledge will do him no good. He will be the same lazy, shiftless, fickle-minded, intractable being that he was before."

In 1883, the Franciscan Sisters of Perpetual Adoration, a religious order with Bavarian roots, arrived in Odanah. With help from tribal members, who constructed a six-room log house, the nuns established St. Mary's School. The school received considerable financial support from the Bureau of Catholic Indian Missions and was also endorsed by tribal leaders, including the Catholic chief, Jean Baptiste Denomie. The Catholic school had a pronounced effect on its Protestant rivals, whose enrollment declined. Within a few years, the Presbyterian headmaster lost his government salary and was forced to close his school.

The corruption that existed elsewhere on the Ojibwe reservations was rampant at Bad River, where the Stearns Lumber Company held a monopoly on the timber contracts and a stranglehold on the tribal economy. The "Octopus," as an *Odanah Star* newspaper editorial called Stearns, owned three sawmills, the blacksmith shop, an icehouse, a barbershop, twenty-five miles of railroad track, and of course the "company store." Throughout the Allotment Period, Bad River tribal members complained that their Indian agent, Samuel Campbell, was

Joe Stoddard ricing on the Bad River Reservation, 1941.
WHi(X3)35386

In 1996, Ojibwe warriors (Ogichida) blockaded train tracks on the Bad River Reservation. The protest prevented a train from carrying sulfuric acid to the White Pine Copper Mine in Michigan's Upper Peninsula.
Photo courtesy of Great Lakes Intertribal Council

conspiring with the Stearns company to cheat tribal members, arranging timber contracts for his Indian charges that were sometimes three times lower than the fair market value.

A federal audit that led to Campbell's eventual dismissal revealed that the Indian Agent kept more than $30,000 of Indian timber money in a personal account at Northern National, a bank controlled by Stearns and other lumber companies. The Ashland account paid two percent interest, unlike accounts in which permanent Indian trust monies were held, which paid five percent. In 1906 a Chicago newspaper revealed that Campbell had made loans to Stearns from this account at little or no interest, enabling the lumber giant to buy the timber rights for more Indian allotments. The result of this "grafting," according to the *Chicago Record-Herald,* was "the protection and fostering of the interests of the banks and lumber companies [rather] than the interests of the Indians." By the end of allotment, the Bad River Band had lost more than forty percent of its original land base.[13]

Sokaogan (Mole Lake)

During the dispersal of the Ojibwe from Madeline Island, an advance party of Indians traveled southward to the area today bordered by Pelican, Metonga, and Pickerel Lakes. There they found a region with abundant rice near present-day Rhinelander. The Ojibwe who returned with them found not only rice but also ample game, waterfowl, and forests filled with maple for sugar and birch from which they made canoes and containers.

Ki-chi-waw-be-sha-shi, Mole Lake leader. Courtesy of Fred Ackley and Fran VanZile

Under the leadership of Ki-chi-waw-be-sha-shi (The Great Marten), the Post Lake Band, as it became known, grew to about seven hundred members. Ki-chi-waw-be-sha-shi matured into a powerful war chief, and his band was recognized as the eastern vanguard of the Ojibwe, protecting the "eastern door" of the nation from enemy attacks. In 1806, the horrendous "Battle of Mole Lake" took place between the Sioux and the Ojibwe, the last large-scale conflict between the two nations over control of the rice beds. In 1999, Charles Ackley, the hereditary chief of the Sokaogon Ojibwe, recounted his grandmother's story about hearing the fierce sounds of hand-to-hand combat from a trench where the Ojibwe women and children lay hidden. "That battle killed more than 500 Indians—both Chippewa and Sioux." The casualties were buried together in a mass grave still tended by Sokaogon elders today.

After Ki-chi-waw-be-sha-shi's death, his son Migiizi (The Great Eagle) assumed leadership of the band. Migiizi's daughter, Ma-dwa-ji-wan-no-kwe, married Williard Leroy Ackley, the first white settler to the area. For reasons that are unclear, Migiizi was prevented from attending the treaty council in 1854 and instead sent his speaker, Ni-gig, to observe the session. Although he was not authorized to negotiate any agreements, Ni-gig signed the treaty instrument. The next year, according to oral accounts, Migiizi met with the treaty commissioners and elicited a promise that twelve square miles of land in the Summit, Pelican, Metonga, and Pickerel Lakes area would be set aside as a homeland for the Sokaogon Ojibwe. It is said that two copies of the map were made, one for the chief and one for the government files. According to Sokaogon oral history, the boat carrying the agent sank in the Great Lakes, and the government's copy was lost. That fall, as the Sokaogon followed the deer herd east to the Peshtigo swamps, Bill Johnson, a white trader, grubstaked the hunters against future pelts. When the Sokaogon were unable to pay their debts, oral accounts say Johnson entered Migiizi's lodge and took the map as collateral. Johnson supposedly gave the plat in payment to another man named Straus, who committed suicide. The whereabouts of the map remain unknown.[14]

Lacking proof of their reservation agreement, the Sokaogon were left homeless. In the 1920s, government reports reduced the Post Lake Band to tragic footnotes about "starving and destitute" Indians roaming in Langlade and Forest Counties.

St. Croix

Along with the Sokaogon, the St. Croix Band represents the other "Lost Band" of Ojibwe. After the Ojibwe dispersal, extended families traveled southwest and established dozens of villages along the St. Croix and Mississippi Rivers. Others who became known as the "Mississippi Bands" continued farther west, settling Leech Lake and other communities in present-day Minnesota. Over the years, the inhabitants of the St. Croix River Valley intermarried with Ojibwe who had traveled farther west and, during times of peace, with Dakota Sioux, who had been pushed west after the Battle at Mole Lake. The Ojibwe moved freely between the various communities in a complex kinship network, which contributed to confusion about who the St. Croix were and to which lands they lay claim.

During the 1837 and 1842 treaties, the St. Croix had a distinct identity. The

A St. Croix delegation meets with Wisconsin Governor Emmanuel Phillip on June 19, 1919. The St. Croix, who were left out of the 1854 treaty, remained landless until 1934.

WHS Archives, Name File

signature page of the first treaty identifies chiefs Bizhiki (The Buffalo) and Ka-be-ma-be (The Wet Month), along with three warriors as being "from St Croix river." Five years later, the same chiefs, along with Ai-aw-bens, are listed as signees on the second document. However, in the 1854 treaty there are no signatures from any of the St. Croix chiefs nor any record that they attended the negotiations. In the eyes of the federal government, the St. Croix had ceased to exist.

Explanations about why the St. Croix were left out of the 1854 treaty and denied a reservation have been lost to time. Tribal historians speculate that perhaps Bizhiki acted deliberately, skeptical of any negotiations with federal officials who had not lived up to the promises of the past. Perhaps the St. Croix chief had expected to negotiate his reservation in talks with the Mississippian Bands. During the treaty talks a major split occurred within the Ojibwe Nation. Ojibwe living in Minnesota—the "Mississippi Tribe of Chippewa"—insisted upon arbitrating an agreement separate from that negotiated by the Wisconsin bands, known collectively henceforth as the "Lake Superior Tribe of Chippewa." Whatever the reasons, the St. Croix, like the Sokaogon, became landless and remained that way until the 1930s.[15]

Gus Sharlow, Lac Courte Oreilles Ojibwe, in his World War I Army uniform. Although Native Americans were not citizens and thereby exempt from the draft, many volunteered for military service. In 1924, Congress approved the Indian Citizenship Act, largely because of the contributions of Native Americans who served in World War I.

WHi(X3)37329

Indian Reorganization

The sweeping social reforms of Franklin D. Roosevelt's administration included a major shift in Indian policy as well. A survey of Indian communities across the country, which became known as the Meriam Report (1928), had revealed extreme poverty, poor health, and cultural despair. When the Great Depression (1929–1933) descended upon the United States, the Ojibwe were no more affected than those in the general population. As Edward Denomie, a Bad River tribal member, wryly observed: "It's always depression on an Indian reservation." But better times lay just ahead. In 1934, at the urging of BIA Commissioner John Collier, Congress passed the Indian Reorganization Act (IRA), which effectively ended the assault on Ojibwe land and culture by halting allotment and dismantling the Indian boarding school system. The Ojibwe were given the opportunity to reconstitute their tribal governments and apply for community development monies through a $10 million revolving loan fund.

The Bureau of Indian Affairs also addressed the extreme hardship of the landless "lost bands." In 1936, the St. Croix Ojibwe adopted a constitution and petitioned for 1,750 acres of scattered land parcels in Burnett and Polk Counties. A year later, the Sokaogan Ojibwe followed suit and took possession of 1,680 wooded acres on the eastern shore of Rice Lake in Forest County. The newly created Ojibwe governments bore little resemblance to the traditional political structures of the past and instead reflected mainstream notions about democracy. The tribes were encouraged to adopt constitutions that resembled corporate charters with by-laws rather than statutes and a chairman rather than a chief of state. Still, reorganization offered the Ojibwe the opportunity to culturally reconstruct their communities and plan for the future, albeit under the watchful eye of the Bureau of Indian Affairs, whose ministrations sometimes proved suffocating.

The 1940s and 1950s brought dramatic changes to Ojibwe villages. World War II emptied Native communities of

Left: Lac Courte Oreilles drum, Honor the Earth Pow Wow, 1997.
Photo courtesy of Lac Courte Oreilles Band of Lake Superior Chippewa

Right: James White dances at the Honor the Earth Pow Wow, 1997.
Photo courtesy of Lac Courte Oreilles Band of Lake Superior Chippewa

their able-bodied men. In World War I, even though they were not citizens and could not be drafted, Ojibwe men had volunteered for military service in astonishing numbers. Sixty men alone had enlisted from Lac Courte Oreilles. Their sons, who had been made citizens under the 1924 Indian Citizenship Act, also felt compelled to serve. Of the Ojibwe soldiers who fought in World War II—and some communities reached nearly total participation—three-quarters volunteered for service. For many Ojibwe, it was the first time they had been out of their homelands. The hunting and tracking skills they brought to the conflict were valued, as was their complex language. The Thirty-Second ("Red Arrow") Infantry Division, in which many Wisconsin men served in the South Pacific, made use of Objibwe "code talkers" whose language was totally unknown to their Japanese adversaries.[16]

Like other Indian communities, who sent nearly 25,000 fathers and sons overseas, the Ojibwe experienced the tragedy of war. The Lac du Flambeau Band lost three of its boys, including its most accomplished musician, Joe Sky. His cousin, Reva Chapman, remembered listening to his horn echo across the lake in the evenings: "As old as I am, I've never forgotten that music. . . ." Ojibwe women contributed to the war effort by knitting and sewing for the Red Cross, buying war bonds, and helping to boost food production beyond their needs. In 1942, they marketed hundreds of thousands of pounds of meat, fish, eggs, and vegetables. Although some Ojibwe women moved to urban areas intending to work in defense-related factories, most filled jobs vacated by white women who were awarded those higher-paying jobs.[17]

The postwar period saw a return to the assimilation efforts that predated John Collier's more liberal policies. A new policy known as "termination and relocation" emphasized preparing American Indians for city life. "Reformers" pressured the government to eliminate federal services to tribes. Although the Ojibwe escaped the fate of the Menominee, whose tribal status was actually terminated under this ill-fated policy, they were enticed to leave their reservations and relocate in major cities. Promises that they would receive job training, housing assistance, and social services evaporated, however, and more than one émigré found that "relocation services" amounted to nothing more than a one-way bus ticket to a large city.

Mildred "Tinker" Schuman teaches students how to make leather pouches as part of the cultural curriculum at the Lac du Flambeau Ojibwe School, 1997.

Photo by Patty Loew

Like other urban Indians, they found solidarity and comfort with other tribal Americans in big cities such as Chicago, Milwaukee, and St. Paul. Many found their voice in the "Red Power" movement that emerged in Native American urban areas. In 1968, two Ojibwe brothers, Vernon and Clyde Bellecourt, co-founded the American Indian Movement (AIM) in Minneapolis. In 1971, Lac Courte Oreilles tribal members occupied the site of the Northern States Power Company dam near Hayward that had flooded their rice beds fifty years earlier. As a result of the AIM-supported takeover, the Lac Courte Oreilles received financial compensation and the right to operate the dam.

Three years later, on March 8, 1974, two Ojibwe brothers set in a motion a series of events that would dramatically change Ojibwe history. Fred and Mike Tribble of Lac Courte Oreilles were arrested and charged with violating Wisconsin conservation laws. The two had been caught ice fishing on a lake, off their reservation but in territory on which the Ojibwe claimed treaty rights to hunt and fish. "When they said I was doing it illegally," Mike Tribble recounted, "I took the treaty out of my back pocket and I said, 'No, I'm doing this under treaty rights.'"

This was by no means a simple poaching incident. The arrests prompted a class action suit against the State of Wisconsin by the Lac Courte Oreilles, who accused state officials of systematically preventing the Ojibwe from exercising their rights to hunt, fish, and gather in the ceded territory as set down in the 1837, 1842, and 1854 treaties. Eventually the five other Ojibwe bands joined the suit. Initially, a federal judge ruled against the tribe; however, in January 1983, the U.S. Seventh Circuit Court of Appeals reversed his decision. Later that same year, the U.S. Supreme Court added some closure—at least temporarily—by declining to review the case.

The following year, when the Ojibwe began spearing fish in off-reservation lakes, they were met by angry protests. Thousands of anti-treaty demonstrators, organized by groups such as Stop Treaty Abuse (STA) and Protect American Rights and Resources (PARR), used political pressure, legal action, and civil disobedience to prevent tribal members from spearing walleye. By 1989, the confrontations had turned violent. On the water, tribal spearers faced rock throwing, boat swamping, and even gunshots. On land, their friends and relatives, who had come to the landings to support them, faced a torrent of racist abuse. Signs bearing such vitriolic messages as "Save a walleye, spear an Indian" and effigies of speared Indian heads led to Wisconsin being described in the media as the "Mississippi of the North."

In the late 1980s, thousands of non-Indian protesters converged on northern Wisconsin boat landings to protest the exercise of off-reservation treaty rights by the Ojibwe. Although many of the protesters argued on the basis of political and legal issues, racism was an unmistakable undercurrent in many of the protests.
Photo courtesy of News from Indian Country

The Ojibwe and their supporters borrowed heavily from civil rights workers who had earlier registered African-American voters during the Freedom Summer of 1964. Several thousand "witnesses" from treaty support groups underwent training and learned nonviolent strategies. They traveled in caravans to northern destinations, identified themselves by wearing white armbands, and collected information for use in police reports, court proceedings, and civil rights investigations. Like the Freedom Riders, witnesses found local police support inconsistent. It was not until the Ojibwe won injunctive relief in federal court that the protests at the boat landings died down.

Between 1987 and 1991, federal court rulings defined and limited the scope of Ojibwe treaty rights and helped shape the manner in which the tribe exercised them. After Judge Barbara Crabb ruled in the Western District Federal Court that the tribe—not the state—had the right to regulate its off-reservation treaty activities, the Ojibwe created the Great Lakes Indian Fish and Wildlife Commission (GLIFWC) to oversee their harvests and provide biological expertise to the bands. Following state and tribal input, a 1989 decision established harvest levels and imposed safeguards to protect the fishery resource. A year later, Judge Crabb issued a decision that extended the Ojibwe deer hunting season and set rules for trapping. However, the Ojibwe did not win on all legal points. In 1991, Judge Crabb ruled that the Ojibwe did not have the right to harvest timber commer-

In 1997 the Mole Lake Ojibwe spearheaded statewide protests against a proposed sulfide mine in Crandon. The tribe feared the mine would pollute the environment and harm their wild rice beds.

Photo courtesy of *Potawatami Traveling Times*

cially—a ruling state officials viewed as a major victory. That same year, she issued a summary judgment and allowed both sides the opportunity to appeal. When neither did, a contentious and expensive seventeen-year legal battle finally ended. In 1999, in a case involving the state of Minnesota, the U.S. Supreme Court ruled definitively to reaffirm the rights of the Lake Superior Ojibwe to hunt, fish, and gather on ceded lands in Minnesota, Michigan, and Wisconsin.[18]

Apart from the treaty rights struggle, perhaps the most significant change that occurred in Ojibwe Country was the expansion of gambling. In 1987, Wisconsin voters approved creation of a state lottery, a Class III gaming activity, which offered opportunities for Indian tribes within the state. The statewide referendum inadvertently presented opportunities for Indian tribes within the state. Federal law allows Indian nations to offer casino-type gambling on their reservations (and, in special circumstances, off the reservation) if the state in which they reside allows Class III gaming. Therefore, beginning in the early 1990s, the Ojibwe opened casinos on all six of their reservations with varying degrees of success.

Coach Damon Sweet-Panek (left) and the Red Cliff youth lacrosse team, Red Cliff Reservation. After a sixty-year absence, lacrosse returned to the reservation as an organized sport in the summer of 2000.
Photo courtesy of Debbie Kmetz

St. Croix's casinos, located across the border from the Twin Cities, have been very profitable. The casino at Red Cliff, the northernmost Ojibwe community and the most isolated geographically, has enjoyed only limited financial success.

The Ojibwe have used the proceeds from their gaming concessions to dramatically improve the quality of life on their reservations. In Red Cliff and Mole Lake, gaming created jobs and funded tribal programs. At Bad River, gaming dollars helped erect new tribal offices and a lodge with meeting rooms and a swimming pool. At Lac du Flambeau and Lac Courte Oreilles, casinos have helped improve education. The Lac du Flambeau built a new elementary school; the Lac Courte Oreilles made improvements to their K-12 school and funded the Lac Courte Oreilles Community College. In the Danbury and Hertel areas, the St. Croix used their gaming money to buy back some of their ancestral land.

The political and legal successes of the bands, along with the infusion of gaming dollars into depressed tribal communities, have given the Ojibwe a new sense of optimism. Housing and social programs have improved. Some communities are beginning to build economic infrastructures designed to last if and when their casinos close. All the Ojibwe bands have put a portion of their gaming profits into environmental programs, administered locally or through the Great Lakes Indian Fish and Wildlife Commission. Each band, for example, runs its own tribal fish hatchery and restocks not only lakes within its borders but also lakes throughout the ceded territory. Other programs include habitat enhancement, sea lamprey control, and shoreline improvement. Given the cultural importance of wild rice, it is not surprising that the Ojibwe annually reseed more than six tons of wild rice into dozens of existing rice beds and are working with state and federal officials to reestablish historical rice stands. Preservation of the "Food that Grows on Water" is of vital importance to the Ojibwe as they look seven generations into the future. In the solemn words of the tribe's Seventh Generation Philosophy: "As those that walked before us provided for the well-being of today's people, so must we think of who will walk the Circle in many years to come."[19]

6 Potawatomi

POTAWATOMI

2001 population: 1,153
1913 Land Purchase: 14,439 acres
1978: 14,439 acres (11,267
  tribally owned)
1999: 12,280 acres (11,560
  tribally owned)

Potawatomi oral tradition tells of three brothers: Ojibwe, the oldest, was the Faith Keeper; Odawa, the middle brother, handled trade; Bodewadmi, the youngest, kept the Sacred Fires lit. Today, within this "family" of Ne shna bek (or Anishinabe)—the ancient confederacy of Ojibwe, Ottawa, and Potawatomi—the Potawatomi still refer to themselves as the "Keepers of the Fire."[1]

When the Ne shna bek left their homes on the eastern seaboard between 500 and 1400 B.P. and moved back to the Great Lakes, the people divided their duties along traditional lines. The Ojibwe carried the sacred scrolls associated with the Midewiwin (traditional religious ceremonies), the Ottawa organized hunts and conducted trade, and the Potawatomi carried and tended the fires. Each responsibility was essential to the group's spiritual, cultural, and physical survival. The three "brothers" may not have had distinct tribal identities during the migration. However, within a century of their return to the Great Lakes region, they had evolved into separate (albeit closely aligned) nations.

Sometime prior to 1500 A.D., the Potawatomi migrated again, this time to the shores of Lake Michigan. Over the next hundred years, they established more than a dozen villages between the present-day Michigan cities of Ludington and St. Joseph. Although much of their food continued to come from hunting, fishing, and gathering, they began to rely more heavily on farming and incorporated corn, beans, and squash into their diet.

The Potawatomi organized their village structure along patrilineal clans, although Potawatomi children were also closely linked to the families of their maternal grandfathers. This provided a wider kinship network and strengthened bonds between villages. Potawatomi always married outside their clans, often intermarrying with Ojibwe and Ottawa. These intermarriages reinforced the Three Fires alliance and offered an added measure of protection to Potawatomi

Top: Potawatomi at Skunk Hill (Power's Bluff) in Wood County, 1930. Skunk Hill is an important spot for gathering special medicines that grow in a unique "closed canopy" forest ecosystem.
WHi(X3)47230

Right: Potawatomi at Skunk Hill, 2000. The Forest County Potawatomi have resisted the efforts of the Wood County Board to allow selective logging on Skunk Hill.
Photo courtesy of *Potawatomi Traveling Times*

families and villages, who could depend upon these kinship ties during times of military threat or stress.

The mode of transportation the Potawatomi brought with them from the north was useful for navigating the waters of their new home. Unlike their neighbors who relied on slower dugout canoes, the Potawatomi used lightweight canoes made of birch bark, which were faster in the water and easier to carry on land. The canoes served them well in warfare and trade—two activities that would dominate Potawatomi affairs during the next two centuries.[2]

By the early 1600s, the Potawatomi had heard rumors about the activities of pale-skinned newcomers with "Hairy Faces" to the east. The Ne shna bek recount that they were living on present-day Washington and Sugar Islands off the Door County Peninsula.[3] In 1634, upon learning of Jean Nicolet's impending diplomatic visit to the tribes of the western Great Lakes, the Potawatomi met him near present-day Green Bay. European trade goods acquired from other tribes were beginning to make their way into the Potawatomi economy. Tribal members were eager to trade directly for items such as metal knives, iron kettles, cloth, beads, and especially firearms. According to oral history, the price of a coveted gun was "beaver skins piled as high as a long-barreled musket."

No doubt the intense intertribal warfare that had erupted in the east convinced the Potawatomi of the usefulness of European firearms. Conflicts between the Five Nations (Haudenosaunee) Confederacy and their competitors over resources and trade agreements sent dozens of tribes fleeing west. By the 1650s, some of the refugees, including the Sauk, Mesquakie, Mascouten, Miami, and Potawatomi had pushed their way into Ho-Chunk and Menominee Country and established a fortified village they called "Mitchigami" on the eastern shore of the Door Peninsula.

After the annihilation of the Huron by the Five Nations in the late 1640s, the Potawatomi took over the role of intermediary, brokering trade between the weakened French and the tribes of the Great Lakes. They filled their canoes with furs, lashed them together in flotillas, and fought their way past Haudenosaunee warriors to Montreal. The Five Nations responded by attempting to nip the trade threat at its source. Beginning in 1653, Haudenosaunee warriors, armed with Dutch- and English-made muskets, mounted three campaigns against Mitchigami. However, the Potawatomi and their allies, who were equipped primarily with bows and arrows, repelled each attack.

In 1701, after the Haudenosaunee signed a peace treaty with the French, many of the refugee tribes returned to their homes in the east. Although the Potawatomi were swept into conflicts between the French and the Mesquakie Nation, the tribe enjoyed a few decades of relative prosperity. By this time, the

Potawatomi had settled more than fifty villages between northwestern Ohio and northern Illinois and controlled an area of nearly 300 million acres. The extent of their influence made the Potawatomi important political and economic allies of the French. Decades of intermarriage between French traders and Potawatomi women bound the two nations in kinship as well.

The Potawatomi were staunch allies of France during the French and Indian War (1754–1763). Potawatomi warriors fought along three fronts: in the east, attacking English settlements from New York to Virginia; in the southeast, battling tribes allied with the English, including the Cherokee; and in French Canada, defending French outposts such as Quebec and Montreal. The Potawatomi were instrumental in several major battles, including one in 1755 in which they helped ambush and rout General Edward Braddock's force near present-day Pittsburgh.

The Potawatomi suffered tremendously with the defeat of the French. Years of British naval blockades had cut off the supply of trade items on which the Potawatomi had become dependent. The Potawatomi needed trapping equipment and ammunition in order to acquire pelts to trade. Unlike the French, the British declined to give gifts or extend liberal credit to their Indian trading partners. Even worse, they raised prices and restricted the supply of some essential items, such as gunpowder. The Potawatomi were not alone in their frustration.

In 1763, the Ottawa war chief Pontiac organized a pan-Indian revolt intended to drive out the British and restore the French. In May, allied warriors from tribes as far north as Lake Superior and as far south as the Gulf of Mexico attacked fourteen British forts. The Potawatomi led successful assaults on Fort St. Joseph's and Fort Michilimackinac and participated in the siege of Fort Detroit. Although the rebellion fizzled, the British had learned a valuable lesson. They restored many of the French trading practices and even hired Frenchmen to conduct trade at some British forts. As a result, the Potawatomi reconciled with the British and once again enjoyed a free flow of trade items.[4]

The Potawatomi's decentralized political structure, which emphasized the autonomy of individual bands, was evident in tribal decisions during the American Revolution (1775–1783). Some bands remained neutral; others joined the war on the American side. Most Potawatomi, however, fought with the British. Like other tribes in the Ohio Valley, the Potawatomi grew increasingly concerned about white encroachment west of the Appalachian Mountains, which the British government appeared willing to stop. In order to secure Indian loyalties following Pontiac's Rebellion, the British had issued the Proclamation of 1763, which forbade white settlement west of the Appalachians. American colonists, however, ignored the edict and began trespassing into Indian Territory.

The Treaty of Paris (1783), in which Britain recognized American independence, made no mention of Britain's Native allies or their concerns about illegal white settlement. The American government viewed the tribes of the Ohio Valley as conquered enemies and made no attempt to control the flood of white settlers. Alarmed at the threat, the Potawatomi joined a pan-Indian alliance of more than a dozen tribes and two thousand warriors. In 1791, under the leadership of the Miami war chief Little Turtle, confederated warriors annihilated Arthur St. Clair's army along the Maumee River. It remains the single worst American military defeat by Indians.

Four years later, however, the Potawatomi were on the losing end of the Battle of Fallen Timbers, which crushed the power of the Ohio tribes and opened the Northwest Territory to white settlement. Although the Potawatomi were pressured to sign the Treaty of Greenville (1795), they were not—as other Ohio Valley tribes were—forced to make land cessions. However, it was a portent of things to come. Between 1803 and 1805 the leaders of various Potawatomi bands signed treaties that ceded portions of Ohio, Indiana, and Illinois. In 1807 the Potawatomi were forced to cede the southeast portion of Lower Michigan.

It is not surprising that a powerful messianic movement that emerged among the Shawnee found great favor among the Potawatomi. Tenskwatawa, a religious visionary who became known as "The Prophet," preached a return to traditional tribal values. He admonished his followers to reject white customs, religions, alcohol, and trade items that fostered dependency. His brother, Tecumseh, a Shawnee war chief, reinforced his brother's spiritual doctrines and added his own: Indian land was owned in common; no tribe had the right to sell a birthright that belonged to all.

Beginning in 1806, followers of The Prophet began visiting Potawatomi communities, inviting them to attend a series of councils at The Prophet's village along the Auglaize River in western Ohio. Over the next year, support for the two Shawnee brothers grew among the Potawatomi—so much so that Main Poc, a noted Potawatomi war chief, invited The Prophet to move his village into Potawatomi Country. Using Prophetstown—as the village became known—as a base, Tecumseh began visiting tribes throughout the Ohio Valley and Great Lakes, encouraging them to join an alliance that would challenge the Americans and resist further surrenders of land by Native people.

By 1810, nearly three thousand Indians from more than a dozen tribes had flocked to Prophetstown. Young Potawatomi warriors, in particular, enthusiastically responded to Tecumseh's call. However, Tecumseh believed that he needed the support of the Cherokee, Chickasaw, Choctaw, and other southern tribes if he was to successfully confront the Americans. In August 1811, when Tecumseh was away recruiting in the southeast, seven hundred allied warriors—a majority of them Potawatomi—attacked William Henry Harrison's troops as he moved them into position near Prophetstown. Harrison repelled the Indian offensive and then counterattacked, burning Prophetstown and destroying Indian crops.

Lacking provisions for the winter, Prophetstown refugees stepped up raids against white settlements in hostilities that melded into the War of 1812. After the debacle at Prophetstown, Tecumseh reorganized his multitribal military alliance and offered help to the British. Together, they successfully attacked American-held forts in present-day Chicago, Detroit, Green Bay, and Mackinac.

Potawatomi Family at Skunk Hill in Wood County, 1920. A ceremonial site, burial ground, and place to gather traditional medicines, Skunk Hill has remained culturally significant to the Potawatomi.
WHi(X3)35356

Not all Potawatomi, however, supported Tecumseh or the British. Some, like the bands near the cities of present-day Milwaukee and Peoria, leaned toward the Americans. However, in the confusion over loyalties, it was difficult to remain outside the fray. In retaliation for the assault on Fort Dearborn (Chicago), for example, the Illinois militia mistakenly attacked the village of Black Partridge, a Potawatomi chief who was friendly to the Americans. Ironically, on the day of the attack Black Partridge was away, attempting to rescue a relative of the American Indian agent at Peoria. Eventually, nearly all the Potawatomi bands that fought did so on the side of the British.[5]

The last great challenge to American expansionism east of the Mississippi died with Tecumseh, who fell in October 1813 at the Battle of the Thames in Ontario. Following the battle, many Potawatomi slipped through American lines and returned to their villages. Their way of life was about to change dramatically. Over the next eight years, the Potawatomi were forced to cede portions of their homelands in four states. In a treaty signed in Chicago in 1821, however, federal negotiators pressured the Potawatomi into giving up nearly all of southern Michigan and a strip of land in and around the south end of Lake Michigan, including Chicago and Milwaukee. White expansion was so rapid, Chief Metea complained, "The plowshare is driven through our tents before we have time to carry out our goods and seek another habitation."[6] Treaty after treaty, parcel after parcel, the Potawatomi sold off their homelands. By 1829, the tribe had ceded about seventy percent of its original land base.

Poverty was an underlying factor in the decision to sell their lands. The Potawatomi had become increasingly dependent upon European trade goods. As their homelands diminished, bands became isolated from each other. White farms and fences dotted the landscape. The Potawatomi had become accustomed to French credit, which allowed them to run up debts in the winter and pay them back with pelts in the spring. The shrinking land base, however, had made hunting less productive. The Potawatomi accumulated massive debts, which the Americans were only too happy to allow them to pay off in land.

The lack of central government placed the Potawatomi at a distinct disadvantage in treaty negotiations. Individual bands handled their own bargaining, sometimes selling land that did not rightfully belong to them. Indian agents sometimes "appointed" chiefs who did not have the authority to sign treaties or speak for tribal members. There were other divisions within the tribe. Years of intermarriage between Potawatomi women and European traders produced great numbers of mixed-blood Indians. Some of these "marginals," as one historian described them, represented an elite class of Potawatomi who used education and the favor of American officials to exploit tribal resources for personal gain. In a letter to President John Tyler, old chief Padegoshek complained that these "half-breeds," as he called them, "claim exemption from . . . your laws—professing to be *Indians*—and at other times claim the protection of them—because they are *whites*."[7]

In the late 1820s, a combination of greed and fear led western expansionists to push the Potawatomi from the last of their homelands. White lead miners had overrun the Fever River Valley in southwestern Wisconsin and northern Illinois, trespassing on lands claimed by the Ho-Chunk, Potawatomi, and other Indians and brutalizing the rightful owners. In 1827, the Ho-Chunk war chief, Red Bird, ambushed a barge carrying mining supplies and raided several settlements near Prairie du Chien. The attacks left several white residents dead. Although the Potawatomi declined Red Bird's invitation to join the raids, this local uprising cast suspicion on the Potawatomi and provided justification—in the eyes of white miners—for the government to force the tribe to part with its lands in the lead district.[8]

On the national level, momentum was building for a plan to move all Indians living east of the Mississippi River to lands set aside for them in the west. After 1830, when President Andrew Jackson signed the Indian Removal Act, all treaties with the Potawatomi would include not only land cessions but also removal from their ancestral lands.

In the Treaty of Chicago in 1833, the Potawatomi signed away the last of their lands east of the Mississippi River. The negotiations reflected how isolated from each other and disparate the bands had become. Chief Simon Pokagon, who along with his band had converted to Christianity, fought removal and was allowed to remain in his village along the St. Joseph's River in Michigan. Another two thousand Potawatomi from southeastern Wisconsin and northern Illinois reluctantly agreed to move, but instead of heading west, they fled to northern Wisconsin and Canada. The bands from northeastern Wisconsin, however, were adamant about remaining in their homelands. After the treaty, they returned to their villages along Lake Michigan and lived unmolested until 1862, when the Sioux Uprising in Minnesota sparked panic among white settlers in Wisconsin toward all Indians. Potawatomi living in the Milwaukee area feared reprisals and forced removal west. Some Potawatomi families moved farther north or hid in the forests. Landless, they became known as the "Strolling Bands of Potawatomi."[9]

Among the Potawatomi who made the trip west, the removals became known as the "Trail of Death." The forced removal of Chief Manomin's (also known as Menominee) Band in 1838, which claimed five or six lives each day, was particularly brutal. According to oral history, Potawatomi warriors were placed in chains and leg irons, crammed in wagons, and denied food and water until the end of

Potawatomi women, circa 1900. From left, Martha Philemon, Eve Sahfenais, Sarah Sahfeinais.
WHi(X3)18847

each day's march. Any tribal member caught trying to slip food or water to them was severely punished. However, a small number of refugees under the leadership of Chief No-zha-kum managed to escape. No-zha-kum led them to Mexico, where they took refuge among the Kickapoo and participated in the Mexican siege of the Alamo in 1836.[10]

Along with the pressure to give up land, the Potawatomi also faced pressure to give up their traditional customs and religions. The Potawatomi had met French Jesuits as early as the 1600s and had accommodated this new religion. During the treaty period, however, they encountered Christian missionaries of many more denominations. Potawatomi treaties often stipulated the construction of mission schools and churches, which were viewed by federal negotiators as necessary to assimilate the Potawatomi.

Like other Ne shna bek, Potawatomi children were often sent to boarding schools, where school officials forbid them from speaking their language and discouraged them from practicing their customs or religious rituals. Masters of accommodation, the Potawatomi responded differently to these pressures. Many accepted Christianity. Others incorporated Christian doctrines into their own belief system. Some Potawatomi created spiritual sanctuaries with other Indians and secretly practiced their own rituals. George Amour grew up in one such hybrid settlement—the McCord Indian Village near the southern end of the Willow Flowage in present-day Oneida County. He described McCord as a place "where many disenchanted, disempowered people from the Midewiwin and Big Drum societies began to gather into a village setting." Made up mostly of Potawatomi and Ojibwe, but also home to a smattering of Menominee and Ho-Chunk, McCord was a refuge where "they could enjoy some economic stability and continue the practice and preservation of their religion, customs, and tradition."[11]

By the beginning of the twentieth century, the Potawatomi were scattered across seven states. The Strolling Bands in northeastern Wisconsin were especially isolated and impoverished. Because of their refusal to move west, they had been denied land and annuities. An inferior Indian boarding-school education had mainly prepared them to join the underclass. Potawatomi women became domestic servants for white families. Potawatomi men found work as day laborers or lumberjacks. Entire families sometimes hired themselves out as migrant workers, picking potatoes and berries for white farmers and canneries. A few eventually managed to save enough to buy back bits of their homeland and acquire homesteads.

In 1909, an enclave of 457 Potawatomi were living near Laona in Forest County. Incredibly, despite the land loss and pressure to assimilate, these Strolling Bands of Potawatomi had never lost their political structure, their language, or their tribal identity. When a U.S. Senate committee arrived to hear their grievances in the fall of 1909, few of the Potawatomi spoke English. In traditional fashion, they preferred to have their chief speak for them. Chief Kish-ki-kaam told the senators that his people wanted land in one piece. They were willing to have it allotted, but they wanted the land placed in trust "so that nobody can get it away from you." They had observed how the allotment process had worked with other tribes and had noted the massive land loss because of foreclosures. When asked if the Potawatomi were in agreement about having allotted land together,

Agnes Menomin watches as her parents pick potatoes near Stone Lake, 1925. In the early twentieth century, itinerant farm work was an important source of income for the Potawatomi.

Photo courtesy of Milwaukee Public Museum; neg. 48652

the chief attempted to steer the questioning back to the tribe's most pressing concern: "We want to know about the taxation," he told them.[12]

The chief's wish that the land be contiguous was not granted. The Potawatomi were allowed to buy only scattered parcels, most of it cutover and rocky. In 1913, these "Strolling Potawatomi" officially became the Forest County Potawatomi Community. The tribe bought its 11,444-acre reservation between Crandon and Waubeno in Forest County with money promised in the 1833 treaty. According to an agreement with the government, the land was allotted in forty- and eighty-acre parcels and would be held in trust for twenty-five years, after which tribal members would be allowed to sell it.

Just before the trust period expired, however, Congress passed the Indian Reorganization Act (IRA) in 1934, which ended many of the federal government's onerous assimilation efforts. The IRA stopped the practice of allotment and phased out the federal boarding schools. It also allowed tribes to reconstitute their tribal governments. The Potawatomi were not permitted to reinstate their clan chiefs or traditional political structure, but instead were forced to adopt the mayor-council model of white government. Still, with the adoption of a tribal constitution in 1937, the Potawatomi at last possessed a refuge in their traditional homeland. The population began to grow steadily as other landless Potawatomi gravitated to the new tribal sanctuary.

The period between 1945 and 1955 brought profound change to the Potawatomi, and, to some, prosperity. Many Potawatomi men volunteered for military service and left Wisconsin for the first time. A few Potawatomi women migrated to Milwaukee and other large cities to take jobs in the defense industry—or, in many instances, to take the jobs vacated by white women who had gone to work in munitions and other factories.

The urban migration that began during World War II continued after the war, fostered by federal programs that reversed Roosevelt's efforts and once again sought to assimilate Native Americans. By means of the disastrous policy known as "termination," the government tried to free itself from its obligations to Indian people. It withdrew financial support from tribes, such as the Menominee, that enjoyed modest economic stability, stripping them of their official status as Indian tribes. Although the Potawatomi were too economically insolvent to be suitable targets for termination, tribal members did feel the effects of "relocation," a related policy.

Under relocation, the government intended to create incentives, such as job training, employment help, and housing assistance, so that Indians would move from their reservation to the cities, where they would find jobs and assimilate into white mainstream society. The reality for most Potawatomi, however, was a one-way bus ticket to Milwaukee or Chicago and directions to run-down housing.[13]

Nevertheless, the resilient Potawatomi accommodated these changes in their status and lifestyle. Many worked in the cities during the week and returned home to the reservation on the weekends. They formed pan-Indian relationships with other urban Indians and, in their own way, re-created—in contemporary fashion—the clan and family networks that had served them well in years past. During the turbulent 1960s, they raised their voices and demanded that government officials address the poverty, substandard housing, and educational inequities both on the reservation and in the cities.

The 1970s brought modest improvements when federal officials ended termination and reversed government Indian policy yet again. President Richard Nixon fostered a new era of self-determination in which the Potawatomi were encouraged to oversee many of their own programs and take over functions previously performed by the Bureau of Indian Affairs. This not only presented new political opportunities for the Potawatomi, it promoted new economic opportunities as

Marge Stevens, an Oneida parent volunteer, teaches a class at the Indian Community School of Milwaukee, Inc., 1971. The school, which formally opened in 1970, receives strong financial support from the Potawatomi Nation. ICS encompasses forty classrooms in eleven buildings on a nearly twelve-acre site in downtown Milwaukee. Photo by Robert Nandell; WHi(X3)35353

well. In 1988, the federal government formally granted the Forest County Band of Potawatomi reservation status.

Of all the changes since the Forest County Potawatomi acquired their reservation in 1913, gaming perhaps has been the most profound. In the late 1980s, the tribe signed a compact with the State of Wisconsin in which it established a casino just north of Carter and a bingo hall on its ancestral lands in the heart of Milwaukee's industrial Menomonee Valley. The gaming facility with its attendant restaurant and theatrical venues in Wisconsin's most populous city has been extremely successful, generating millions of dollars in profits.

For the first time, the Potawatomi have been able to diversify their economy and build an infrastructure. The tribe constructed a hotel and conference center adjacent to its casino in Carter and other tribally owned or supported businesses, including a heavy equipment excavating and construction company, a logging cooperative, a combination "smoke shop" and craft store, a convenience store, and a gas station. It recently established a red deer herd to provide venison to wholesalers, retailers, and restaurants.

In November 2000, the Potawatomi opened a new $120 million gaming complex in Milwaukee's Menomonee Valley. The facility features 75,000 square feet of gaming space, two concert halls, and five restaurants.
Photo courtesy of Potawatomi Bingo Casino

The 1999 Forest County Potawatomi Thunderbirds. Pop Warner football is just one of the youth sports sponsored by the tribe's recreation department.

Photo courtesy of *Potawatomi Traveling Times*

In addition to its economic enterprises, the Potawatomi subsidize the Indian School of Milwaukee with financial support that exceeds $20 million a year. Open to children of all Indian nations, the school offers a culture-based curriculum that not only promotes academic excellence but also builds pride and respect for traditional tribal values. Reservation-based educational programs include Head Start and Even Start, a multifaceted program that focuses on academic, physical, social/emotional, cultural, and spiritual skills.

Other programs include a self-insured medical, dental, and mental health care plan administered from the tribe's health and wellness center built in 1995, a daycare center completed in 1995, a senior center, and services to the elderly, such as transportation, housing, home repair, and home-delivered meals. The tribe also operates a housing program for tribal members and a newspaper, the *Potawatomi Traveling Times*.[14]

The Potawatomi Nation's self-stated vision for the future is rooted in a commitment to provide for its 1,000 members, half of whom reside on the reservation. It hopes to improve housing, much of which is still substandard. It has set a goal of full employment for tribal members who are able to work. Through its gaming operations it indirectly supports more than 30,000 jobs, the vast majority of which are held by non-Indians. It has created an energetic environmental department in order to improve and protect its physical landscape. In this manner, the Potawatomi see themselves strengthening the cultural landscape.

Above: Kayla Christjohn (left) and Precious Torres, students at the Indian Community School of Milwaukee, Inc., display their exhibit at the 1999 American Indian Science and Engineering Society (AISES) Regional Science Fair at the Milwaukee Public Museum.
Photo by Andrew Connors

Left: The Potawatomi Historical Center and Museum, near Crandon, houses tribal archives and cultural artifacts.
Photo by Patty Loew

In 1998, the Potawatomi became the first Indian nation in Wisconsin to share gaming revenues with another tribe. Fittingly, the recipient of their generosity was a member of the Ne shna bek Alliance, the financially strapped Red Cliff Band of Ojibwe.[15] In their success, the Potawatomi believe they have not forgotten the ancient obligations that bind them politically and culturally to their Ne shna bek family. "Bodewadmi"—Little Brother—continues to fulfill his nurturing role as "Keeper of the Fire."

7 Oneida

When the Oneida first encountered Europeans, they occupied an area of at least six million acres in present-day New York State. They were part of the Haudenosaunee, or "People of the Long House," meaning the Five Nations Confederacy, which also included the Seneca, Cayuga, Onondaga, and Mohawks. Later, when the Tuscarora joined in the 1720s, they became the Six Nations Confederacy. Europeans sometimes referred to them as the "Great Iroquois League" or the "Iroquois Confederacy." However, *Iroquois* is not a Haudenosaunee word. Rather, it derives from the French corruption of a derogatory Huron word, meaning "Black Snakes."[1]

The Oneida refer to themselves as the *On^yote:aka*, meaning "People of the Standing Stone." According to oral accounts, the name derives from the practice of the Oneida people to move their villages every ten to fifteen years. At each new location, a large, upright stone appeared. Oral tradition tells of a time prior to the formation of the Confederacy when the Haudenosaunee fought with each other in an endless cycle of violence. Hiawatha, the Great Peacemaker, visited their villages and delivered the Great Law of Peace: "Together you are like the five fingers of a warrior's hand," he told them. "United you are powerful; divided you are weak."[2]

Although some western historians speculated that the Haudenosaunee formed their league as late as the sixteenth century, in response to the European threat, Oneida oral history is clear that the Five Nations Confederacy was founded long before European contact. From its formation until the late eighteenth century, the League was the most powerful political system in North America.

Fifty councilors or chiefs chosen by the clan mothers made up the Grand Council, which was composed of an unequal number of representatives from

Menominee ceded land for New York Indians in 1831.

1831

Oneida Reservation

Present Oneida Reservation created in 1838.

ONEIDA

2001 population: 13,508
1838 Treaty: 65,000 acres
1978: 2,581 acres (2,108 tribally owned)
1999: 6,340 acres (5,846 tribally owned)

Wampum, made from whelk shells, not only represented currency but also was used to convey messages.
WHi(W63)23,528

each tribe: fourteen Onondaga, ten Cayuga, nine Oneida, nine Mohawk, and eight Seneca. A complex voting system prevented one nation from exerting more political power than the others. The chiefs, selected on the basis of their political and spiritual strengths, guided the five nations during times of peace. When the Haudenosaunee faced outside threats, war chiefs took charge. The League was a confederacy in the truest sense. Each tribe was free to pursue its own national interests, which it did from time to time.[3]

By the seventeenth century, the Oneida lived in large villages—at least two communities, but possibly as many as nine—in the eastern United States, mostly in modern-day New York and Pennsylvania. There were also Oneida living among other Haudenosaunee, especially the Tuscarora with whom they were especially close.

The first documented Oneida encounter with Europeans was not a positive one. In 1615, Samuel de Champlain, who had established Quebec six years earlier, participated in raids with the Huron against the Haudenosaunee. Most likely it was an Oneida village that Champlain and his allies attacked. During a three-hour battle, Champlain's men set fire to the village and killed a number of its defenders. Fifteen members of Champlain's party were wounded, including Champlain, who took arrows in the leg and knee. The next recorded encounter came in late fall of 1634 when a Dutch physician visited the Oneida. Dutch traders had sent Harmen Meyndersten van den Bogaert to investigate reports that the French had been trying to initiate trade among the Oneida. He described the Oneida village in this way:

> This castle [village] is also located on a very high hill and was surrounded by two rows of palisades, 767 steps in circumference, in which there are 66 houses; but built much better and higher than all the others. There were many wooden gables on the houses, which were painted with all sorts of animals. They sleep here mostly on raised platforms, more than any other Indians. . . . I saw houses with 60, 70 and more dried salmon."[4]

What van den Bogaert described was a typical Haudenosaunee village with dozens of Long Houses surrounded by a defensive palisade. The palisade consisted of two or three rows of posts set in the ground—a formidable barrier that encircled the entire village. The Long Houses, which varied in length between forty and two hundred feet, were built of long saplings about two to three inches in diameter. Workers thrust each sapling into the ground and then bent it forward, making a "hoop" that they secured in the ground opposite to form two outer walls and an arched roof. They created vertical end walls by lashing more saplings to the roof, leaving doorways at each end. Once they had constructed the frame, they fastened sheets of elm bark, resembling large shingles or slates, to the structure.

The floor plan provided compartments for individual families and fireplaces in the central aisle running the length of the Long House. Sleeping platforms adjoined the house walls with storage at either end of the house. The entire dwelling represented an extended family, or matrilineage, whose clan symbol—a wolf, bear, or turtle, for example—appeared above the door. A man marrying an Oneida woman moved into his wife's Long House, and their children became members of her clan.

The Oneida were principally agricultural people, raising corn, beans, and squash using "slash and burn" agricultural methods. This involved burning off the ground cover, planting crops, and rotating the fields when the land lost its fertility. The women made decisions about the land, worked the fields, and gathered

Oneida women, circa 1900. The Oneida, members of the Six Nations Confederacy, are a matrilineal community, meaning clan membership is determined by the mother's lineage.
WHi(X3)20037

roots, berries, and nuts. The men supplemented the diets of the community with game and fish. The Oneida also "deer farmed" by burning underbrush, and sometimes the forest trees themselves, to create the necessary deer browse.[5] When the Oneida depleted the firewood or exhausted their garden soil, they moved. They also relocated their villages for defensive purposes and to eradicate disease brought by Europeans.

Strong spiritual beliefs, expressed in the traditional teachings of the Long House, united Oneida communities. Other religions, including Gaiwiio, a post-contact vision introduced by the Seneca prophet Handsome Lake, reinforced their cultural and spiritual bonds with other Haudenosaunee. The arrival of European diseases, however, would greatly test these belief systems. Within a few decades of encounter, perhaps as many as 1,800 of the 4,000 Oneida had died from smallpox, influenza, measles, and other diseases for which they had no immunity.

Like other Haudenosaunee communities, the Oneida participated fully in the fur trade, aligning themselves economically with the Dutch and later the British against the French and their economic allies. Their French partners included principally the Algonquian nations but also the Huron, a tribe related linguistically to the Oneida but not a member of the League. Attempts by both the Huron and the Haudenosaunee to monopolize trade erupted in the Beavers Wars (1624–1697), which sent dozens of tribes fleeing westward.

By 1649, with flintlock rifles acquired from the Dutch, the Haudenosaunee had asserted their military might and extended their economic and political influence to nearly all of their neighbors. These included many Indian nations beyond the St. Lawrence River to the north, southward to present-day South Carolina, and westward as far as the Mississippi River. Tribes who wished to participate in the Haudenosaunee trade network were allowed to "come in under the wing" of one of the original Five Nations.

The Haudenosaunee then turned their attention to other tribes, including the Anishinabe—Ojibwe, Potawatomi, and Ottawa—who had moved to fill the intermediary position vacated by the Huron. When the Anishinabe attempted to send flotillas of furs by canoe up the St. Lawrence to Quebec, they met fierce resistance from Haudenosaunee warriors. The League often dispatched—not always successfully—large war parties into the Great Lakes to cut off trade at its source. In 1655, for example, an allied force of Ojibwe, Ottawa, and Nipissing defeated a large war party of Oneida and Mohawks on the eastern shores of Lake Superior.

The Five Nations were skilled in the art of economic diplomacy. After the Dutch departed, the Haudenosaunee quickly incorporated British trade items into their network, supplanting French items that were often more expensive and less well-made. In this way they weakened the French economically. At the same time they used British fears about French influence among the Algonquian tribes to manipulate Great Britain diplomatically. For example, the Haudenosaunee persuaded the British to coax their Indian allies, such as the Cherokee, Choctaw, Chickasaw, and Creek Confederacies, into becoming allies, convincing them that it would diminish French political power in the Southeast.

Occasionally divisions arose within the Haudenosaunee, especially after Christianity was introduced. The Haudenosaunee practice of adopting large numbers of enemy tribal members into the nation after a military defeat promoted factionalism, because many of these subdued Indians had converted to Catholicism. In 1667, the Jesuits persuaded a few Christian Oneida families to settle near their mission at La Prairie in the St. Lawrence Valley. The soil was not suitable for corn, however, so the families moved from La Prairie to a new village,

Caughnawaga. This group, initially made up of Oneida but later dominated by Mohawk Christian families, became a major French ally. For the next hundred years, the Caughnawaga danced a precarious dance, fighting with the French against the English, but withdrawing when Haudenosaunee allies joined the British in fighting against the French.[6]

Other Christian missionaries arrived in Oneida territory, including Samuel Kirkland, a member of the Missionary Society of Scotland. Kirkland worked among the Oneida for forty years, preaching a gospel of farming, prohibition, and religious-based education. His goal was to instill in the Oneida the skills that would let them succeed in what was becoming a white, European-dominated society.

The years of the American Revolution were pivotal for the Oneida and the other members of the Confederacy. In 1775, concerned about the disunity that was erupting between England and the American colonies, the Haudenosaunee sent a delegation to Albany to meet with representatives appointed by the Continental Congress. American officials did not ask for the Confederacy's help, but rather asked it to maintain its neutrality, promising, as Britain had done, to continue to trade with the League.

By this time, however, pro-American and pro-British factions had developed within the League, which had now expanded, with the addition of the Tuscarora, to become the Six Nations Confederacy. Joseph Brant, an influential Mohawk leader educated in Britain, was very pro-British, as was his sister, Mary, who had married William Johnson, the British Indian agent. Brant persuaded the Mohawk, Seneca, and Cayuga to secretly support the British. Individual Oneida, such as Honyere Doxtator, however, aligned themselves with the Americans. Doxtator collected a number of Oneida warriors and offered his services to a company of white militiamen. Other Oneida and Tuscarora served as scouts, runners, and intelligence gatherers for the Americans.

In 1777, the League officially ruptured. At Brant's urging, the Mohawk, Seneca, and Cayuga agreed to join the offensive against the Americans. The Oneida and smaller numbers of Tuscarora and Mohawk accepted a war belt to help the Americans. Their contribution was considerable. The Oneida helped break the siege of Fort Stanwix and distinguished themselves at the Battle of Oriskany in 1777. Doxtator's wife, Dolly Cobus (also known as Polly Cooper), fought alongside the men at Oriskany, where she loaded her husband's musket for him after he was wounded and fired her own weapon against the enemy.[7]

During the winter of 1777, at Valley Forge, the Oneida supplied George Washington's troops with six hundred bushels of corn and other provisions. Later, in Philadelphia, Dolly Cobus cooked for Washington and his staff but declined payment for her services. As a thank you, the Continental Congress appropriated funds to buy a black shawl that Cobus had admired—a gift that has been passed down from generation to generation and is still owned by members of the Oneida nation.[8]

Despite their loyalty during the American Revolution, after the war the Oneida faced hostility from their white neighbors and the skullduggery of unscrupulous developers, including the Ogden Land Company, which claimed to hold preemptive rights to much of the Haudenosaunee land. In 1785 and again in 1788, New York officials forced the Oneida into a series of fraudulent leases that transferred more than 5.5 million acres of Oneida land to the state. The New York compacts directly violated terms of the Treaty of Fort Stanwix (1784), which confirmed Oneida ownership of their lands. Subsequent treaties negotiated with the state after 1790 and adoption of the Trade and Intercourse Act, which held that only the federal government had the right to negotiate Indian treaties, were invalid. The words of Good Peter, an Oneida chief, articulated the depth of Oneida despair over the loss of their land: "The voice of birds from every quarter cried out you have lost your country—you have lost your country! You have acted unwisely —and done wrong."[9] It was during this anxious and chaotic time that a powerful and perplexing agent of change emerged.

Eleazer Williams was born into a mixed-blood Mohawk family at Caughnawaga in about 1787. Baptized Catholic but educated by Congregationalists, Williams accepted a position offered by the Episcopal Church as missionary to the Haudenosaunee. In 1816, Williams arrived to begin his ministry and within a few years began laying plans for an ecclesiastical "Grand Iroquois Empire" somewhere west of Lake Michigan. With money from the Ogden Land Company and encouragement from the U.S. War Department, New York State officials, and Foreign Missionary Society, Williams began exploring a land purchase from the Menominee and Ho-Chunk Nations.

In 1821, Williams accompanied a delegation of Oneida and other New York Indians to Green Bay and asked for an eighteen-mile-long, four-mile-wide strip of land along the Fox River north of Lake Winnebago. Under pressure from the United States government, the Menominee and Ho-Chunk agreed. The following year, Williams returned with a larger delegation and attempted to extend the land purchase to six million acres. The Ho-Chunk "absolutely refused and withdrew from the council." The Menominee, who later complained that they misunderstood the terms of the treaty, agreed to allow the New York Indians to share the land as joint occupants.

In 1824, about one hundred Oneidas and an equal number of Mohicans, who had sought refuge with the Oneida in New York some years earlier, arrived in

Eleazar Williams, an Episcopal missionary of Mohawk descent, accompanied a delegation to Green Bay in 1821 and returned the following year with a larger contingent of Oneida who settled along the Fox River.
Sketch by George Catlin; WHi(X28)1078

Wisconsin and settled along the Fox River. The following year, another 150 families joined them and both groups created a permanent settlement at Duck Creek. However, the migrations did not have universal support within the Oneida community. In a letter to President James Monroe, Oneida chiefs representing those who intended to stay in New York complained that Williams was "scheming" with land speculators and was a "tool" of the Ogden Land Company. They disputed his claim of $10,026.43 for "services" and argued that he was not authorized to remove the New York Indians.

As pressures continued in the east, however, Oneida continued to emigrate to the area west of Lake Michigan. "With the loss of land there was most certainly a loss of the natural environment needed to support the Oneida people both culturally and economically," wrote twenty-first-century Oneida historian Carol Cornelius. The Oneida who remained in New York knew the implications of heavy logging by white settlers: "The trees provided the natural environment for plants, animals, fish, and medicines which Oneida people utilized on a daily basis." Many Oneida believed that the only chance for survival was in the west.[10]

By 1838, more than 650 members of the tribe were living at Duck Creek, planting corn, potatoes, and turnips on about four hundred cleared acres. The successive waves of émigrés reflected different religions and different political philosophies. The early arrivals were primarily Episcopalians belonging to the First Christian Party, as they described themselves. The next group tended to be Methodists who belonged to the so-called Orchard Party, later known as the Second Christian Party. Later arrivals were "pagan," or traditional people.

The Menominee had never accepted the treaty terms that brought the New York Indians to their homeland, and, in 1831, they negotiated a treaty with the United States that reduced the Oneida land holdings to 500,000 acres. No Oneida were present at the treaty session. In the Treaty of February 3, 1838, the First

Christian and Orchard Parties negotiated their own agreement with the United States that officially established the reservation boundaries, awarded unequal sums of money to each party, and set aside one hundred acres of land for each tribal member—a total of 65,400 acres. Although the land was to be held in common, Oneida who migrated from New York to Wisconsin after 1838 were not recognized as being entitled to share in the ownership of the reservation. These Oneida, known as the "Homeless Band," remained landless until 1891.

A heavy influx of white immigrants into the Green Bay area in the 1840s and 1850s placed new pressures on the tribe. The American Civil War years (1861–1865) brought prolonged droughts, early frosts, and periodic outbreaks of smallpox. One hundred thirty-five Oneida men—about ten percent of the total Oneida population of 1,300—volunteered for duty with the Union Army. They paid a terrible price: Only fifty-five of the volunteers returned from the war.

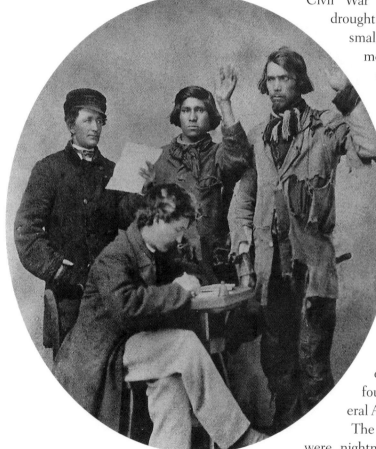

"New York Indians," most likely Oneida and Mohican, being sworn into Civil War service.
WHi(X31)10058

Shortly after the war, the Oneida began talk of another removal farther west or allotting the reservation as a means of providing property for the landless Oneida who had arrived from New York and Canada after the 1838 treaty. Thirty-year-old Cornelius Hill, a Bear Clan chief who in 1903 would be ordained an Episcopal priest, led a successful fight against removal. However, the community deeply divided on allotment, which began in 1891, four years after Congress passed the General Allotment Act.

The results, as elsewhere in Indian Country, were nightmarish. Unfamiliar as they were with white people's concept of taxation, many Oneida lost their lands by failing to pay their taxes. Others fell victim to the unscrupulous practices of various land companies. By the 1930s, less than five percent of the original reservation remained in the hands of Oneida tribal members.[11]

Oneida members of the Grand Army of the Republic (Civil War veterans) outside Parish Hall on the Oneida Reservation, circa 1907

WHi(X3)40387

In 1934 the Indian Reorganization Act (IRA) officially ended allotment and allowed the Oneida to reorganize their tribal government. Under provisions of the act, however, U.S. officials pressured the tribe into writing a constitution and adopting a white form of government at the expense of the tribe's traditional clan council of chiefs.[12] The U.S. government bought back nearly 1,300 acres and placed it in trust for the Oneida Nation. The IRA also ended other policies of forced assimilation, such as government boarding schools.

The educational experience for Oneida children had been a mixed one. Although the Episcopal and Methodist Churches operated schools on the reservation, many Oneida children were sent to faraway government schools, including Carlisle in Pennsylvania and Hampton in Virginia. Both the church schools and the government schools emphasized the use of English and discouraged the expression of Oneida culture. "When I went to school, they used to punish us if we spoke Indian," a seventy-two-year-old Oneida woman remembered. Many parents, wishing to protect their children from the harsh treatment they had endured, encouraged their children to adopt white ways. "They [my parents] were shamed into not teaching history," said another. "My mother and father both spoke Oneida, but [not so much] in front of us kids."[13] The result was a decline

Girls in the Oneida Indian School laundry room. Indian schools typically offered a half-day of academics and a half-day of industrial training.

Photo courtesy of Milwaukee Public Museum; neg. A-621-4C

in the usage of the Oneida language skills and a forcing underground of traditional Oneida cultural practices. It also led to a scattering of the Oneida people. Although some tribal members found jobs in the white communities that now surrounded them, many of the best-educated Oneida moved off the reservation and never returned.

During World War I, 150 Oneida men were among ten thousand Indians who volunteered for active duty, even though many were not citizens. In World War II, more than seventy percent of Oneida men enlisted and more than two hundred were killed. Because of the complexity of their language, Oneida men were used as "code-talkers" by the U.S. Army's 32nd Infantry Division, which fought in New Guinea and the Philippines. Oneida women supported the war effort by buying war bonds and moving to urban areas and taking jobs in defense-related industries. A few even enlisted in the military.[14]

After the war, Oneida continued to migrate to urban areas, particularly Milwaukee, and experienced what other relocated Indians experienced: substandard housing, marginal jobs, and cultural disconnection. Under the leadership of several Oneida, however, the pan-Indian community constructed a kinship network that amounted to a home away from home—a kind of urban reservation—that provided a patchwork of social services under the auspices of various church and government organizations. The Oneida, perhaps better equipped to deal with urban life because of the proximity of their reservation to Green Bay, took leadership roles in the pan-Indian and Red Power organizations that emerged in Milwaukee during the late 1960s and early 1970s.

Oneida boys pick berries during a school outing.
Photo courtesy of Milwaukee Public Museum; neg. A-621-1

The 1980s were a momentous decade for the Oneida. As one of the first Indian tribes to sign a gaming compact with the State of Wisconsin, the Oneida became a textbook example of how to use casino dollars to successfully create an infrastructure. Today the Oneida Nation owns a convention center, including a hotel, restaurant, and multimedia auditorium. Other holdings include convenience stores, "smoke shops," a promotional products distributorship, a seven-thousand-acre farm, an electronics firm, and a thirty-two-acre business park in

Aerial view of the "Turtle" School at Oneida. The shape of the school invokes the Oneida creation story, in which the earth is created on Turtle's back. Photo courtesy of George W. Brown, Jr., exhibit, Ojibwe Museum and Cultural Center, Great Lakes Intertribal Council

Brown County.[15] In addition to its commercial interests, the tribe operates a public museum and library, provides health services, housing, utility services, and nearly one hundred other programs to its members. One of its most stunning successes is the Oneida Tribal School. The school, built in the shape of a turtle—symbolic of the Hauden-os-aunee Creation Story—offers kindergarteners through eighth-graders a culture-based curriculum. Its stated mission is to "illustrate and reflect the world as it is, as it has been, and as it can be in the natural presence of Mother Earth and all living and non-living inhabitants." The Oneida Nation also offers early childhood, Head Start, high school, and higher education opportunities to its tribal members. Moreover, the financial stability of the Oneida Nation has permitted it to repurchase 11,000 acres of its original reservation.

The government is slowly reversing the two-hundred-year-old wrongs committed upon the tribe. In 1985, the U.S. Supreme Court ruled that state officials had acted illegally in dispossessing the Oneida of 270,000 acres of land in New York and ordered them to pay damages. (As of 2001, New York officials have yet to compensate the tribe.) Thorny issues remain, including the rights of white property owners in the ceded territory and how those rights can be reconciled without compromising the sovereignty of the Oneida Nation.[16] Still, a political, economic, and cultural renaissance is underway in Oneida Country, propelled by a growing income stream and rooted in traditional Haudenosaunee values.

8 Mohican Nation Stockbridge-Munsee Band and Brothertown Indians

Menominee
Reservation

Mohican
Reservation

Mohican
1831-1848

Brothertown
1831-1839   Mohican
1831-1839

*Menominee granted land
to Mohican and Brothertown
in 1831. Mohican moved to
present reservation in 1856.*

**MOHICAN NATION
STOCKBRIDGE-MUNSEE
BAND**

2001 population: 1,500
1856 Treaty: 44,000 acres
1978: 15,320 acres (3,450 tribally
  owned)
1999: 16,200 acres (16,044 tribally
  owned)

BROTHERTOWN

2000 population: 2,568
1838 Treaty: 23,000 acres
1839: Tribal status terminated
1999: Landless

Muh-he-con-nuk, the name Mohicans give themselves, translates to "Great Waters that Are Never Still," a reference to the Hudson River—not their original homeland, according to oral tradition, but similar to the land they had left.[1] According to Mohican oral history, the tribe emigrated "from the west by north of another land." They crossed waters "where the land almost touched." At the time of European contact in the early seventeenth century, the Mohicans occupied the Hudson River Valley north to Lake Champlain, east to the Westfield River, and west to Schoharie Creek near present-day Albany, New York. The Dutch apparently thought Muh-he-con-nuk was too difficult to pronounce and called them *Mahican,* the word for "wolf" in the Mohican language and one of the tribe's three principal clans. The Mohicans spoke an Algonquian dialect and are linguistically related to most of the Great Lakes tribes, among whom they would settle in the nineteenth century.

The Mohicans occupied as many as forty villages in New York, each fortified by a palisade that enclosed and protected about two hundred inhabitants. Tribal members lived in wigwams—circular structures made of bent saplings and elm bark—or Long Houses, which sheltered several families of the same clan. As often as necessary, the Mohicans moved their villages in order to locate near fresh garden soil. The Mohicans were gardeners who practiced polyculture, intercropping corn, beans, and squash together with sunflowers. Women did the gardening; men provided fish and game. Mohican towns were headed by sachems selected on the basis of heredity and matrilineal descent and advised by a council of clan leaders.[2] The principal clans were designated the Bear, Wolf, and Turtle. The sachems met regularly in the main village of Shodac, east of Albany, to discuss civil matters. In times of war, the sachems passed leadership to a war chief chosen on the basis of his proven ability. During military crises, his authority was absolute.[3]

James Fennimore Cooper's misidentification of the tribe in *The Last of the Mohicans* has confused many people. Cooper was actually writing about the Mohegan, a tribe that inhabited present-day eastern Connecticut. His character Uncas, for example, was a real figure in Mohegan history. Indeed, the two tribes may have been one people before contact, but they had distinct identities by 1609 when the English explorer Henry Hudson encountered the Mohicans. An account of that meeting, published in the early twentieth century, in which the Mohicans supposedly presented Hudson with a "covenant chain shining with beaver's grease" is viewed with skepticism by contemporary tribal historians. They agree that covenant chains came considerably later, although they acknowledge that the beaver trade commercially linked the two cultures until the 1670s.[4]

The Mohicans, who could marshal about a thousand warriors out of their total population of eight thousand at the time of contact, became a formidable ally of the Dutch. The Dutch practice of taking Native slaves had alienated many of the coastal tribes, but the Mohicans, who lived far enough inland that they had not had that experience, were eager to trade. After Hudson returned to Holland aboard his fur-laden ship, the word spread that the Mohicans were willing and friendly traders. The next few years saw a tremendous influx of Dutch settlers into Mohican territory.

Like the tribes of the Great Lakes, the Mohicans quickly adapted to the fur trade and incorporated European trade items into their

John Quinney, Stockbridge Indian and sachem, during the Mohican Nation's migration west to Wisconsin in the 1820s.

Portrait by Amos Hamlin; WHi(X3)45435

economies: guns, ammunition, copper kettles, knives, axes, scissors, and liquor, particularly rum. Because of their strategic location and their close proximity to Dutch trading centers, the Mohicans exerted great influence over the trade in wampum, the purple and white whelk shells that served as the principal monetary exchange in North America until British and American silver replaced it in the eighteenth century.

Initially, European trade brought prosperity to the Mohicans. In time, however, it fostered economic dependence and fed hostilities between the Mohicans and their nearest neighbors, particularly the Mohawks. The flashpoint in relations between the Mohicans and the Mohawks came in 1624, with the construction of Fort Orange by the Dutch. Trade intensified because of the new fort, and the two Indian nations quickly exhausted the supply of fur-bearing animals in their countries. When the Dutch approached the Mohicans and asked them to facilitate trade with other Algonquian tribes to the north, the Mohawks attacked the Mohicans. Fighting quickly spread to allies of the two nations, and although the Mohawks and the Mohicans arranged a truce in 1628, the conflict—known as the Beaver Wars—continued sporadically between the Haudenosaunee and the Algonquian until nearly the end of the seventeenth century. The Haudenosaunee prevailed. As part of the peace agreement, the Mohicans were forced to pay the Mohawk a quantity of wampum each year and to serve as mercenaries in Haudenosaunee raids against tribes to the south.[5]

Even more than war, European diseases took a deadly toll on the tribe's population, which dwindled to less than a thousand. The conflicts with the Mohawk and white encroachment pushed the Mohicans from their homeland. By 1724, the Mohicans were reduced to two villages along the Housatonic River in Massachusetts.

By then—ravaged by warfare and disease, their ancestral lands reduced, their power threatened on all sides—the Mohicans were vulnerable to the messages of missionaries who arrived in their communities. Many became Christians. They were particularly interested in the British god because, as one Mohican sachem put it, "we see that he doth better to the English than other gods do to others."[6] In 1734, the Mohicans agreed to host a Calvinist mission in a village they called "the Great Meadow," known to the Europeans as "Stockbridge." Within a few years, several hundred Pequots, Wappingers, and other converted Indians settled there. Although the Mohicans formed the core of the community, to white settlers, they and the other Christianized Indians began to lose their distinct tribal identities and became known simply as the Stockbridge Indians.

During this time, the Mohicans began intensively to reconstruct their culture. The tribe found itself surrounded by fences and boundary lines. Unable to pick up and move when their garden soil was exhausted, as had been their tradition, the Mohicans borrowed farming methods from their white neighbors. Some worked as farmhands and lumberjacks. Others moved into skilled trade positions. Mohican men frequently began hiring themselves out as mercenaries, providing military support to the British against the French. Mohican women moved through the countryside, selling handmade baskets, wooden bowls, brooms, and moccasins.[7]

Mohican culture absorbed white culture. Most tribal members replaced wigwams with frame houses and buckskin with cloth. Heavily influenced by Christian missionaries, Mohican families shifted from a matrilineal to a patrilineal focus. They worshipped in churches and sent their children to school. They were also drawn into the imperial conflicts of white colonists.

Unlike their allies, the Shawnee and Delaware, who were trying to drive the British out of the Ohio Valley, most Mohicans supported the British during the French and Indian Wars (1754–1763) and Pontiac's Rebellion (1763). The Mohicans suffered great risks during these conflicts, and the threat of massacre was never far off. When Indian families fled their settlements in fear, whites moved in and took over their homes and farms. After the Mohicans returned, the white squatters refused to leave. At the request of the tribe's sachem, Daniel Nimham traveled to England to seek redress from King George III, and British officials promised to help return the lost land to the Mohicans. But the coming of the American Revolution delayed any action.

The Mohicans entered the war on the side of the Americans. They fought in the siege of Boston and at Bunker Hill. Mohicans served as scouts at Saratoga and in numerous other battles. In 1778, Nimham himself was killed at the Battle of Kingsbridge. The tribe's losses during the war were devastating. Half its fighting men were killed, and of those who did return, many found that white intruders had moved onto their lands and into their homes. Mohican loyalty to the United States was largely repaid with hostility and theft.[8]

The bleak future that loomed for their Stockbridge settlements forced the Mohicans to look for a new home. When the Oneida, who had also fought on the side of the Americans, invited them to live in their nation, the Mohicans accepted. In the mid-1780s, the Mohicans packed up and resettled near Oneida Lake in upstate New York—the first migration that the "Many Trails People" would endure. They settled on land that had been given by the Oneida to an amalgamated group of Pequot, Mohegan, Niantic, Tunxis, Wangunk, and Montauk Indians who had named their new settlement Brothertown and who had collectively became known by that name. In 1802, after the Mohicans extended a similar offer

Samson Occom, religious leader of the Brothertown Indians during the migration west to Wisconsin in the 1820s.

WHi(X3)33206

to a band of Christianized Delaware Indians living in New Jersey, the Delaware moved north to join them.

Toward the end of the eighteenth century, the Brothertown had consolidated under the leadership of Samson Occom, the first Indian formally trained as a Christian minister and a descendant of Uncas, the grand sachem of the Mohegan. In order to escape the influence and pressures of white settlers, Occom led his followers to refuge among the Oneida. Like the Mohicans and the Oneida, the Brothertown prospered until a series of fraudulent treaties and illegal land leases forced all three tribes to move.[9]

In 1818, two groups of Mohicans led by John Metoxin and Joseph Quinney left New York, traveling overland and sometimes by water to the White River area in present-day Indiana to live among their friends and relatives, the Delaware Munsee. The two groups traveled separately and took different routes—a trip that took many months. Metoxin's sixty or seventy followers wintered in Piqua, Ohio, but by the time they arrived in Indiana, the Delaware had been forced to sell their holdings and were preparing for removal father west to lands in southwestern Missouri. In 1821, Eleazer Williams, an Episcopal missionary, secured a portion of Menominee and Ho-Chunk land for the New York Indians. The Mohicans of Stockbridge, the Munsee, and the Brothertown decided to accompany him far to the west, to the Upper Great Lakes region.

Between 1822 and 1829, groups of Mohicans arrived in what is today east-central Wisconsin. The first émigrés settled at Grand Cackalin (known today as Kaukauna) on the Fox River. Controversy over the land sale, however, led to new treaty negotiations, and in 1834 the Mohicans and Brothertown Indians moved again to new lands along the eastern shore of Lake Winnebago.

Meanwhile, momentum was building in Washington to remove all the Native peoples living east of the Mississippi River to territory west of the Mississippi. Passage of the Indian Removal Act in 1830 created great uncertainty among the Mohicans. "Fearing the inevitable," some Mohicans and a group of Delaware Munsee from Canada asked to move to Indian Territory in 1839. To accommodate them, the tribe's chief sachem, Austin Quinney, negotiated a land cession whereby half of the Mohicans' best land—23,040 acres—was sold to the government in

Mohican blacksmith shop near Stockbridge, circa 1913.
WHi(X3)28385

order to finance the removal of the Mohicans who wanted to move west. About seventy of the 217 Mohicans, along with 100 of the 132 Delaware Munsee, attempted the long, arduous trip. Many died along the way. Some arrived in Oklahoma and were absorbed by other tribes. Others eventually returned to Wisconsin.[10]

The Mohicans' hardship continued through the next decade. In 1843, Congress extended citizenship to the Mohicans, a move that split the tribe into two factions. Some Mohicans accepted citizenship and sold their lands to white developers—or lost their property when they failed to pay their taxes. Others, including John W. Quinney, who was elected grand sachem in 1852, resisted apportionment and refused to cooperate with those who coveted Mohican land.

Under Quinney's leadership, the Mohicans withstood numerous efforts to remove the tribe and alienate the Mohican people from their land. In 1856, the Mohicans negotiated the last of their treaties, which resulted in another move, this time to the townships of Bartelme and Red Springs in Shawano County, which had previously formed part of the Menominee Reservation.[11]

Other Quinneys rose to prominence in the tribe. John Quinney's sister, Electa, became the first female public schoolteacher in what would become Wisconsin in 1848. Born in 1802, Electa Quinney was educated in mission schools in Connecticut and New York. She taught school in New York for six years before her family, along with her tribe, left for Wisconsin. In 1827, the tribe constructed a church and a log schoolhouse modeled after white schools in New York and New England. It was a free school, open to anyone of any denomination. A year later, Electa took over the classroom, and the tribe paid her salary. In a letter to friends back east, she expressed her optimism: "The people have much improved since leaving New York."[12]

Like the Mohicans, the Brothertown Indians initially prospered after their move to Wisconsin, but their fortunes declined in the face of increasing pressure from white settlers. Believing it was the best strategy to retain their land, in 1839 the Brothertown accepted citizenship. Congress passed legislation that established their 23,000-acre reservation as a town and divided the tribe's land holdings into private property that was allotted to each tribal member. At the same time, the act unilaterally usurped the power of the Brothertown Indians to govern their land. It decreed, ". . . their rights as a tribe or nation, and their power of making or executing their own laws, usages, or customs, as such tribe, shall cease. . . ."[13]

Allotment took its inevitable toll, and the Brothertown quickly lost their lands to foreclosures and tax sales. By 1880, many were living with friends and relatives on the Oneida and Mohican Reservations and, if they were lucky, providing day labor in neighboring white communities. Yet, despite their uncertain political status, the Brothertown continued to function as a tribe. They petitioned Congress over land issues and joined a lawsuit with other New York tribes over treaty matters. In 1878, Congress acknowledged the existence of the Brothertown by inviting the tribe to appoint five trustees to oversee the sale of unallotted Brothertown tribal land. A hundred years later, in a struggle to restore tribal status, the Brothertown would argue that these government-to-government relations were strong evidence that both the tribe and the federal government recognized the Brothertown as a tribal entity.[14]

The years following allotment (1887–1934) were extremely difficult for the Mohicans and Brothertown. Timber companies clear-cut the tribes' lush pine forests, leaving a denuded landscape susceptible to erosion and forest fires. The intended transition from lumbering to agriculture did not occur to the extent the government had hoped. Much of the land was not suitable for farming; the soil was thin and sandy, and the growing season was too short. The inability to make a living on the land created considerable hardship, made worse by the Great Depression and a widespread drought during the early 1930s. Edwin Cuish, whose parents had a small farm, remembered a big dust storm "that came all the way from Oklahoma," darkening the sky at midday and smothering their crops. Feed for the family's livestock was so scarce "they had to cut leaves off the trees in order to feed the cows."[15]

By 1934, only 16,000 acres of the original 40,000-acre Mohican reservation remained in tribal hands. In addition to the land deprivation, the Mohicans also experienced the loss of their most precious resource: their children. Mohicans, like other Indian nations, were forced to send their children to boarding schools, where white educators discouraged the use of traditional language and cultural expression. "They tried to erase us," explained Dorothy Davids, who attended the Lutheran Mission School in Red Springs. "They tried to make us into something else." Davids described herself as one of the luckier children. Every Friday afternoon, her grandfather, whose farm on the reservation was adjacent to the school, came to the mission to pick her up and take her home for the weekend. She was among the fortunate ones: Other children stayed at the mission for the entire school year, returning home only in the summers, if at all. Some Mohican children attended schools in Gresham and Tomah, but a few were sent as far away as Flandreau, South Dakota, and Carlisle, Pennsylvania.[16]

The experiences of Mohican children at the mission school were mixed. Bernice Miller Pigeon recalled her years—during the 1920s—as happy ones. She met lifelong friends, including a young Mohican girl from Oshkosh who became her best friend. "Rachel lived in the city. I never would have met her if it wasn't for the school." Like Davids, Pigeon was able to return to her family each weekend. Often she would invite schoolmates who lived far away to spend Saturdays and Sundays with her on her family's farm. As one of ten children she was no stranger to hard work and did not mind the chores to which she and the other children were assigned at school. "My job was to bake. I worked in the bakery one hour every day after classes." She and two other girls baked thirteen loaves of bread each day.[17]

Davids described the school as "not bad" but a place where punishment could be harsh: "I do remember getting thrashed with a cat o' nine tails for some infraction and then walking over to my grandpa's house, sobbing," Davids said. "He marched me back to the school, up the stairs, down the hall, into an office. . . . I don't know what he said to the matron, but I never got thrashed again." Still,

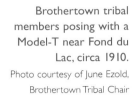

Brothertown tribal members posing with a Model-T near Fond du Lac, circa 1910.
Photo courtesy of June Ezold, Brothertown Tribal Chair

she conceded, "they did teach us to read and write." Davids, who became the first American Indian woman to graduate from the University of Wisconsin–Stevens Point and who later earned a master's degree at the University of Wisconsin–Milwaukee, believes the fundamental skills Indian children learned in boarding schools proved useful. "A lot of leadership emerged from that basis. It doesn't mean they made leaders out of us, but by getting some skills, later we were able to stand up and criticize some of the government's policies."[18]

Federal Indian policy, with its emphasis on eliminating tribal culture and alienating Native people from their land, offered much to criticize. However, that changed in 1934 with passage of the Indian Reorganization Act (IRA). The IRA signaled a new shift in the government's approach toward its Native population, away from the assimilationist policies of the past and toward a recognition that Native culture could be a source of strength and opportunity. Federal policymakers began closing Indian boarding schools and buying back tribal land lost through the allotment process. Under the IRA, the government returned 15,000 acres of land to the Mohicans, which allowed them to rebuild their community. In 1938, the Mohicans reorganized their tribal government and approved a new constitution.

Mohican men, like other Indian men in Wisconsin, enlisted or were drafted into the military during World War II. They served in integrated units, which made their progress difficult to track. Like other Indian people, many Mohicans gravitated to the cities after the war as part of the government's relocation program. By 1966, less than half the Mohicans listed on the tribal rolls were residing on the reservation. Dorothy Davids was living in the Milwaukee area, teaching junior high school students in suburban West Allis. An internship with the National Congress of American Indians in Washington led her to leadership workshops and a job training workers for national poverty programs, including Volunteers in Service to America (VISTA). Her work took her to the American Indian Center in Chicago, where she saw the tragic effects of relocation: "Native people losing their jobs, being evicted, and having a hard time adjusting to urban life. . . ." She remembered being called to a rundown apartment where a woman with a three-week-old baby was in the throes of a breakdown. Davids, who helped the woman commit herself to a hospital, was concerned about leaving the infant with the woman's husband, who had been drinking. "There was a young Navajo woman, newly married, who was washing dishes at the Center, helping out, and I remember saying how worried I was about that baby. And, she said: 'I'll take it.' And you know, she took care of that baby for oh, maybe three weeks, until its mother was out of the hospital." For Davids, the Indian Center was an important link for Native people. "It was a second home, a lifeline."[19]

The quiet work of urban Indian centers, such as the one in Chicago, was overshadowed by the more boisterous and sometimes confrontational activities of the American Indian Movement (AIM), which gained national prominence in the 1960s and 1970s. Armed confrontations and takeovers, such as those at Wounded Knee in South Dakota and the Alexian Brothers Novitiate in Gresham (both 1973), focused national attention on historic injustices and on the problems facing contemporary Native people, such as political corruption, miserable health care, and poverty. "For me, AIM was part of the cutting edge," Davids explained. "But they made the people standing behind them look more reasonable. Without AIM, a lot of the changes wouldn't have occurred." AIM was useful in other ways to activists like Davids who were working within the system. "Lord, all we had to say was, 'I guess we'll just have to call in AIM,' and we usually got what we wanted. It was an exciting time."[20]

The arrival of gaming in the late 1980s ushered in exciting economic times for the Mohicans. In addition to a casino, a "smoke shop" offering tobacco products, and a bingo hall, the tribe owns and operates a golf course, a campground, family and community centers, elder housing, and the impressive Arvid E. Memorial Library Museum. It administers dozens of tribal programs on the reservation, including Head Start, and will open a $5 million health clinic in 2001. "It took smoking and gambling for Indians to get on their feet," Bernice Miller Pigeon observed wryly. "I'm looking forward to when gaming stops. Maybe we'll have other industries to keep us going."[21]

In addition to using their gaming dollars to build an economic infrastructure, the Mohicans have also invested in efforts to enhance the natural and constructed beauty of the reservation. The tribe recently improved Many Trails Park, adding picnic areas and footbridges. It has restored a number of historic stone cottages built by the Works Progress Administration during the 1930s and 1940s. The tribe has used its gaming dollars to create a wildlife and waterfowl sanctuary they call the "Circle of Flight."

Though the tribe is by no means wealthy, the Mohicans are experiencing economic growth unprecedented in three hundred years. Tribal members are returning to the reservation for jobs and opportunities. A sense of optimism is reflected in the cultural renaissance that is underway in the Mohican Nation. Youth drums, pow wows, and artistic expression are beginning to flourish. The past has left an indelible imprint on the tribe, evident in an emblem imprinted on ban-

The Mohicans have been active in environmental protection, including the establishment of a bird sanctuary, "Circle of Flight," on the reservation.
Photo by Patty Loew

ners, jewelry, T-shirts, and tribal letterhead—the "Many Trails" symbol. It reminds them of the traumatic removals and difficult paths that marked Mohican history, but it also encourages them about the possibilities in the journey that lies ahead.

The Brothertown Indian Tribe of Wisconsin, meanwhile, does not "officially" exist. The Brothertown Tribal Council continues to meet monthly in Fond du Lac, and tribal members are optimistic that the federal government will soon acknowledge their status as a tribe. Federally recognized tribes receive financial support and are eligible for federal services. However, many Brothertown Indians say economic stability is just one aspect of the motivation for reestablishing themselves as a tribe. They see federal recognition as an opportunity to strengthen their Indian identity. "We want to preserve our heritage," Brothertown tribal chair June Ezold says. "We want to do this for ourselves and our ancestors."[22] In 1996, the Brothertown filed a formal petition for federal recognition. As of summer 2001, the tribe was still waiting for an official response.

Beyond

The here is reason to be hopeful about the future of the Indian nations of Wisconsin. Yet there remains a sense of uneasiness about the gains tribal governments appear to have made in the era of self-determination that has marked the last twenty-five years of U.S. Indian policy. Legal victories involving treaty rights and the apparent success of gaming in some tribal communities have led to fears about potential white backlash. Although the State of Wisconsin and the eleven federally recognized tribal governments have created successful partnerships in many areas, including health, social service, and natural resource enhancement, an underlying tension still exists, as evidenced by the jurisdictional disputes that frequently surface.

More and more of these disagreements involve environmental issues. Throughout the 1990s, the Sokaogon Ojibwe led efforts to block a proposed copper mine near Crandon in Forest County. The Sokaogon, together with a coalition of environmental groups, successfully pushed for a statewide mining moratorium, arguing that the long-term implications of mining should be fully investigated. In 1999, their neighbors, the Forest County Potawatomi, became only the fifth tribe in the United States to acquire a Class One Air

Young singers at the New Dawn of Tradition Pow Wow, held in conjunction with the Wisconsin Sesquicentennial, August 1998.
Photo courtesy of Great Lakes Intertribal Council

125

Quality designation for their reservation. This stipulation, initially opposed by the state, could have a considerable impact on mining and other land-use decisions within a ten-mile radius of the reservation. Similarly, as the century drew to a close, the Red Cliff Ojibwe were still waiting for a federal ruling on their efforts to halt the commercial harvest of submerged timber along the Lake Superior coast.

In Oneida and Potawatomi Country, local white residents have expressed concern over attempts by the tribes to buy back land within their original reservations and return it to trust status. Indian trust lands, which are not taxable, represent a loss of revenue to municipalities and county governments. In Lac du Flambeau, the tribe's attempts to assess white property owners for roads, which were illegally carved through the reservation decades ago, have produced angry reactions among nontribal residents of the reservation. On every reservation affected by allotment, Indian nations have been asked—as they have since European contact—to accommodate non-Indians who live near or within their borders.

At the close of the twentieth century, the infusion of gaming dollars into Native communities ravaged by years of poverty and neglect began to express itself in better housing, more jobs, and expanded tribal government programs and services, such as the wellness centers operated by the Mohicans and Ho-Chunk. These modest improvements have fed misperceptions that "all Indians are rich," even though Native American communities remain among the poorest in the state.

Along with their modest economic gains, many tribes have experienced a cultural renaissance. Tribal artists have found inspiration in ancient art forms. There is renewed interest in Native languages and traditional activities. At Bad River, for example, Anishinabe attendance of the Three Fires Midewiwin rites quadrupled in the 1990s. Pow wows, such as the Honor the Earth celebration at Lac Courte Oreilles, continue to grow in popularity, and new pow wows are added every year. Overall, a better of quality of life is taking root.

For thousands of years, Native people have greeted each dawn with prayers of thanksgiving and offerings to the Creator. Today, the twelve Indian nations in Wisconsin stand at the daybreak of a new millennium. They endured, and ultimately survived, a long season of darkness. Stronger culturally, politically, and economically than they have been in nearly two hundred years, the Ho-Chunk, Menominee, Ojibwe, Potawatomi, Oneida, Mohican Nation Stockbridge-Munsee Band, and Brothertown Indians confidently greet the dawn of the twenty-first century.

Notes

Chapter 1 Notes

[1] Anthropologist Paul Radin details the Red Horn story in "Winnebago Hero Cycles: A Study in Aboriginal Literature," *Indiana University Publications in Anthropology and Linguistics, Supplement to International Journal of American Linguistics,* Vol. 14, No. 3, July 1948 (Baltimore: Waverly Press, Inc., 1948), 115–136.

[2] Robert J. Salzer, "Chapter 4: Wisconsin Rock Art," *The Wisconsin Archeologist,* edited by Robert A. Birmingham, Carol I. Mason, and James B. Stoltman, Vol. 78, No. 1/2 (Jan.–Dec. 1997), 48–77.

[3] Frances Densmore, *Chippewa Customs* (Minneapolis: Ross & Haines, Inc., 1929; reprint edition, 1970), 88–97.

[4] For more on wampum, see Frederick J. H. Merrill, "Wampum and Shell Articles," *Bulletin of the New York State Museum,* Vol. 8, No. 41 (February 1901) (originally published in 1901; reprinted by AMS Press, New York, 1978), 455–457; and George Hammel, "The Iroquois and the World's Rim," *American Indian Quarterly,* Vol. 16, No. 4 (Fall 1992), 451–470. Carol Cornelius, Director of Oneida Nation Historical and Cultural Department, agrees that white symbolized peace but could not confirm the cultural meanings of the use of black or red wampum. (Phone interview with author, November 2000.) Excellent histories and images of wampum belts are available on the Web. See http://www.nativetech.org/wampum/wamphist.htm, a site maintained by Tara Prindle, a doctoral candidate in anthropology at the University of Connecticut.

[5] Edward Benton-Banai, *The Mishomis Book* (St. Paul: Red School House, 1988), 29–34.

[6] Oneida Nation, from the pamphlet *The Iroquois Story of Creation* (Oneida, Wisconsin: Oneida Nation Culture and Heritage Department, undated).

[7] Ho-Chunk Nation, from the pamphlet *Ca Worak* [*Deer Story*] (Mauston, Wisconsin: Hocak Wazijaci Language & Culture Program, 1997).

[8] The notion that animals helped create the earth is a theme repeated in the origin stories of many Indian Nations. Joseph Bruchac tells a particularly compelling version of the Fisher story in *Native American Stories* (Golden, Colorado: Fulcrum Publishing, 1991), 79–86.

[9] Joseph Bruchac and Michael Caduto have a wonderful collection of stories about the re-

lationship between Native people and plants and animals in *Keepers of the Earth* (Golden, Colorado: Fulcrum Publishing, 1988).

[10] For more on the mound-building and Mississippian cultures, including the settlement at Aztalan, see *The Wisconsin Archeologist,* Vol. 78, No. 1/2 (1997), 141–249 passim; Robert A. Birmingham and Katherine Rankin, *Native American Mounds in Madison and Dane County* (Madison: City of Madison and the State Historical Society of Wisconsin, 1996); and Robert A. Birmingham, "Ancient People of Monona" (unpublished paper, undated).

[11] Benton-Banai, *The Mishomis Book,* 74–78.

[12] Robert Bieder discusses the Menominee and Ho-Chunk clan systems in *Native American Communities in Wisconsin 1600–1960* (Madison: University of Wisconsin Press, 1995), 23–38. The origins of the Ho-Chunk Buffalo Clan are recounted in *The Ho-Chunk and Green Lake* (Black River Falls, Wisconsin: Hocak Wazijaci Language & Culture Program informational sheet, undated).

[13] Barbara A. Mann and Jerry L. Fields, "A Sign in the Sky: Dating the League of the Haudenosaunee," *American Indian Culture & Research Journal,* Vol. 21, Issue 2 (1997), 143.

[14] Carol Cornelius, author interview, Oneida, Wisconsin, September 20, 1999.

Chapter 2 Notes

[1] *Since 1634: In the Wake of Nicolet,* a videotape produced by Ootek Productions, the Educational Communications Board, and the Board of Regents, University of Wisconsin System, 1993. Dave Erickson wrote, produced, and directed the video with assistance from co-producers Lance Tallmadge of the Ho-Chunk Nation and Alan Caldwell of the Menominee Nation.

[2] Jay Miller wrote a concise and very readable general history of the French fur trade era and its impact on the Indian nations of the Northeast and Great Lakes regions in *The Native Americans.* See chapter ten, "The Northeast" in *The Native Americans,* edited by Betty Ballantine and Ian Ballantine (Atlanta: Turner Publishing, Inc., 1993).

[3] Although some western historians speculate that the Ho-Chunk may have been ravaged by a smallpox epidemic, Randy Tallmadge, Hocak (Ho-Chunk) Wazijaci Language and Culture Program, states that the reference to "yellow sickness" was not consistent with tribal descriptions associated with pox. Randy Tallmadge, author interview, Madison, December 10, 1997.

[4] For more on the fur trade and its effects on Indian Nations in Wisconsin, see chapter three of Robert Bieder, *Native American Communities in Wisconsin 1600–1960* (Madison: University of Wisconsin Press, 1995).

[5] Richard White, *The Middle Ground* (Cambridge: Cambridge University Press, 1991). White argues that after encounter, Native communities did not merely assimilate European culture and values but rather intermingled with Europeans to construct "new systems of meaning and of exchange."

[6] *Potawatomi Nation in Canada* (Mactier, Ontario, Canada: Keewatinosagiganing Potawatomi Nation Cultural Council, 33103 [1988]), 26, 47.

7 In his 1852 history of the Ojibwe, William Warren, the son of an Ojibwe mother and English father, complained about "chief making" by the English and Americans. Unlike the French, whom Warren believed did not appoint chiefs "unless being first certain of the approbation of the tribe," the English and their successors awarded medals and presents "indiscriminately or only in conformity with selfish motives and ends." He alleged that this undermined the influence of the hereditary chiefs. William Warren, *History of the Ojibway People* (St. Paul: Minnesota Historical Society, 1885), 135.

8 Simon Pokagon was a Christian clan leader of the St. Joseph's Band of Potawatomi in Michigan. Although most Potawatomi unsuccessfully resisted efforts by the federal government to remove them west of the Mississippi River, Pokagon was able to establish a permanent reservation in Michigan. In a biography written by C. H. Engle, Pokagon issued a diatribe against the use of alcohol. See *O-gî-mäw-kwe mit-i-gwä-kî* (Hartford, Michigan: C. H. Engle, 1899).

9 Alice E. Smith, *The History of Wisconsin, Volume I: From Exploration to Statehood* (Madison: State Historical Society of Wisconsin, 1973). Smith relies heavily on Reuben G. Thwaites, ed., *The Jesuit Relations and Allied Documents: Travels and Explorations of the Jesuit Missionaries in New France, 1610–1791* (73 vols., Cleveland, 1896–1901), Volumes 18 and 23, as well as other nineteenth-century and early-twentieth-century accounts written by American, Canadian, and French historians.

10 Edward Benton-Banai, *The Mishomis Book* (St. Paul: Red School House, 1988), 106.

11 James DeNomie, who has conducted genealogical research over the past decade, supplied the author with a DeNomie (Denomie) family tree during an interview in Milwaukee, Wisconsin, August 1986.

12 See Smith, *From Exploration to Statehood*, 51–56.

13 Thomas Vennum, Jr., provides a fascinating account of the fateful lacrosse game in his fine book, *American Indian Lacrosse: Little Brother of War* (Washington, D.C., Smithsonian Institution Press, 1994), 82–103. In summer 2000, Vennum helped establish a youth lacrosse program on the Red Cliff Ojibwe Reservation, where the game had not been played since the 1930s.

14 Reports of skirmishes between Native people and American frontiersmen likely reached Indian communities in what would become Wisconsin through the trade networks. Alice Smith writes that these frontiersmen, who were floating their goods down the Ohio River and moving their families over the mountain passes, were a "constant threat to the Indian way of life." In offering another explanation for why the tribes of the Great Lakes remained loyal to the British, she points out that the Indians "had few religious, language, or economic ties with the eastern colonists and little inclination to take the rebel side. . . ." Smith, *From Exploration to Statehood*, 69.

Chapter 3 Notes

1 Marshal Pecore, forestry manager, Menominee Nation. The author interviewed Pecore for "Nation Within a Nation," a documentary segment within *Looking for America*, which aired nationally on PBS, October 12, 1998.

2 For more detailed accounts of the Menominee's role in the American Revolutionary War, see Patricia Ourada, *The Menominee Indians: A History* (Norman, Oklahoma: University of Oklahoma Press, 1979), 47–51, and Felix M. Keesing, *The Menomini Indians of Wisconsin* (Madison: University of Wisconsin Press, 1987), 87–90.

3 Tecumseh traveled to Green Bay in 1810 or 1811 and met with Menominee chiefs, including Tomah, one of the most important Menominee clan leaders at the time. Tomah told the Shawnee war chief that he would not prevent individual warriors from joining Tecumseh, but that he himself intended to stay neutral and counseled his tribe to do likewise. "These hands are unstained with human blood," Tomah told Tecumseh. James W. Biddle, "Recollections of Green Bay in 1816–17," *Wisconsin Historical Collections,* I (1903), 52.

4 Grizzly Bear, "Minutes of the 1825 Treaty at Prairie du Chien, August, 1825," *Documents Relating to the Negotiation of Ratified and Unratified Treaties with Various Tribes of Indians, 1801–1869,* in Record Group 75, Records of the Bureau of Indian Affairs (Washington, D.C..: National Archives, 1960), available at the Wisconsin Historical Society as microfilm P97-2750, reel 1.

5 Letter of the Secretary of War, *Wisconsin Historical Collections,* XII, p. 173, quoted in Keesing, *The Menomini Indians,* 130.

6 Russell Horton, "Menominee Braveheart" (unpublished paper, 1999). Horton's paper was one of the finest written during my teaching fellowship in the Department of History at the University of Wisconsin–Madison. Using newspaper accounts, manuscripts, and oral history from David Grignon, Menominee Tribal Historian, Horton reconstructed the events surrounding Oshkosh's ascent to power and his ordeal in court.

7 Treaty of February 8, 1831, Treaty of February 17, 1831, and Treaty of October 27, 1832 (all negotiated in Washington, D.C.), *Documents Relating to the Negotiation of Ratified and Unratified Treaties with Various Tribes of Indians, 1801–1869,* in Record Group 75, Records of the Bureau of Indian Affairs, microfilm P97-2750, reel 1.

8 Ourada, *The Menominee Indians,* 118.

9 Treaty of May 12, 1854, Falls of the Wolf River. *Documents Relating to the Negotiation of Ratified and Unratified Treaties with Various Tribes of Indians, 1801–1869,* in Record Group 75, Records of the Bureau of Indian Affairs, microfilm P97-2750, reel 1.

10 H. H. Chapman, "The Menominee Indian Timber Case History" (proposal typed and bound by or for Chapman, 1957), p. 1. Chapman, a professor Emeritus at Yale University, compiled a history of the legislation and administration of the Menominee timberlands and offered proposals for settlement. In his foreword, Chapman stated that the main purpose of the text was to "emphasize the unsettled character of the Menominee Timber problem and the need for enlightened and constructive action for the benefit not only of the Tribe but of the public and of conservation in Wisconsin." This document was instrumental in the $8.5 million judgment awarded to the Menominee by the U.S. Court of Claims in 1952.

11 Francis Paul Prucha, *The Churches and the Indian Schools* (Lincoln, Nebraska: University of Nebraska Press, 1979), 58.

12 *Ibid.,* 6.

13 *Ibid.,* 10.

14 Deborah Shames, *Freedom with Reservation* (Washington, D.C.: National Committee to Save the Menominee People and Forests, 1972), 10. This is an excellent economic, political, and social history of the Menominee people during the termination years. It is told from the perspective of Determination of Rights and Unity for Menominee Shareholders (DRUMS), an activist group that opposed termination and agitated for restoration.

15 Nicholas C. Peroff, *Menominee DRUMS* (Norman, Oklahoma: University of Oklahoma Press, 1982), p. 56. I am indebted to Ada Deer, former Secretary of the Bureau of Indian Affairs and Menominee activist, who shaped my understanding of Menominee Termination. Her seminar on American Indian issues was one of the first I took when I enrolled in graduate school at the University of Wisconsin–Madison in 1987. As the tribe's official representative in Washington during the termination years, Deer was intimately involved in the negotiations and resolution of Menominee Termination and Restoration.

16 Shames, *Freedom with Reservation,* 26–27.

17 Among the many fascinating items in the archives of the Wisconsin Historical Society are Timothy Ericson's National Guard Papers, 1941–1978. The papers include copies of the unit's newspaper, *The First Battalion Sentinel,* as well as Ericson's account of the Menominee takeover of the novitiate.

Chapter 4 Notes

1 HoChunk Nation Department of Historical Preservation, *The HoChunk Nation: A Brief History* (Black River Falls, Wisconsin: Ho-Chunk Nation, undated). There is some disagreement about the translation of "Ho-Chunk." Ken Funmaker, Jr., former director of the Hocak Wazijaci Language and Culture Program and a fluent Ho-Chunk speaker, states that the literal translation is "People of the Sacred Language," a reference to Ho-Chunk being the parent language of many Siouan dialects. Author interview with Ken Funmaker, Jr., and Randy Tallmadge, Mauston, Wisconsin, November 18, 1997. The tribe has used alternate spellings in its various publications; these include Hocak, Ho-Chunk, and HoChunk.

2 Ho-Chunk Historic Preservation Department, *The Ho-Chunk and Green Lake* (Black River Falls, Wisconsin: Ho-Chunk Nation, undated). References to the Ho-Chunk origin stories are also made in *Thunder in the Dells,* a television documentary co-produced by Dave Erickson and Lance Tallmadge, which aired on Wisconsin Public Television in 1992. *Thunder in the Dells* (Spring Green, Wisconsin: Ootek Productions, 1992).

3 Letter by Joseph Street, Secretary of War, describing talks with Winnebago leaders, January 8, 1828, Office of Indian Affairs, Letters Received, Prairie du Chien Agency, Roll 696, quoted in *Winnebago Oratory* by Mark Diedrich (Rochester, Minnesota: Coyote Books, 1991), 27.

4 The Wisconsin Historical Society's Draper Manuscripts contain "The Tecumseh Papers, 1911–1931," a collection of letters, clippings, and other material assembled by Lyman Copeland Draper for his projected biography of the Shawnee leader. The papers indicate that as early as 1806, Tecumseh began traveling to Potawatomi, Menominee, Ojibwe, and Ho-Chunk communities in an effort to enlist their support for his pan-Indian alliance.

[5] The 175 Ho-Chunk attending the council were represented by two leaders identified in treaty documents as "principal chiefs": Caramine and "De-ca-ri" (probably Decorah). Although the Ho-Chunk were concerned about incursions by white settlers, they appeared to be quite content to continue to share the land with other tribes. Caramine told the American delegation: "The lands I claim are mine and the nations here know it is not only claimed by us but by our brothers the Sacs and Foxes, Menominees, Iowas, and Sioux, they have used it in common. It would be difficult to divide it, it belongs as much to one as the other." His remarks are contained in the "Minutes of the 1825 Treaty at Prairie du Chien, August, 1825," *Documents Relating to the Negotiation of Ratified and Unratified Treaties with Various Tribes of Indians, 1801–1869,* in Record Group 75, Records of the Bureau of Indian Affairs (Washington, D.C.: National Archives, 1960), microfilm P97-2750, reel 1.

[6] Treaty Journal, August 11, 1827, Winnebago File, Great Lakes–Ohio Valley Ethnohistory Archive, Indiana University, Bloomington, quoted in Diedrich's *Winnebago Oratory,* 23.

[7] Thomas L. McKenney, *Memoirs, Official and Personal* (Lincoln, Nebraska: University of Nebraska Press, 1973), 107–8, quoted in Diedrich's *Winnebago Oratory,* 24.

[8] *Black Hawk: An Autobiography,* edited by Donald Jackson (Urbana, Illinois: University of Illinois Press, 1964), 114–115. Antoine LeClair, U.S. Interpeter for the Sacs and Foxes, wrote Black Hawk's "autobiography." Although LeClair maintained that he was "cautious" with the narrative and pronounced it "strictly correct," there remain questions about how much of the narrative was Black Hawk's and how much of it LeClair's.

[9] Henry Dodge to Old Turtle, Spotted Arm, Little Black, Silver, and Man Eater (represented by his sister and her daughter) at Four Lakes [Madison], May 26, 1832, from an article by Milo M. Quaife, "Journals and Reports of the Black Hawk War," *Mississippi Valley Historical Review,* Vol. xii, No. 3 (December 1925), 406.

[10] In 1958, anthropologist Nancy Oestreich Lurie interviewed Mountain Wolf Woman, a Ho-Chunk elder, who told Lurie that "land matters were the exclusive concern of the Bear Clan people who would act in the interests of the entire group." *Mountain Wolf Woman,* edited by Nancy Oestreich Lurie (Ann Arbor, Michigan: Ann Arbor Paperbacks [The University of Michigan Press], 1961), 114.

[11] Erickson and Tallmadge, *Thunder in the Dells.*

[12] Baptiste, "Blue Earth & Crow Creek," from the pamphlet *The Ho-Chunk Removal Period* (Black River Falls, Wisconsin: Ho-Chunk Historical Preservation Department, undated).

[13] Lurie, *Mountain Wolf Woman,* 3.

[14] Ho-Chunk Nation, "Migrant Farm Workers," from the pamphlet *The Cranberry People* (Black River Falls, Wisconsin: Ho-Chunk Heritage Preservation Department, undated).

[15] Ho-Chunk Nation, "Protestant and Catholic," from the pamphlet *The Blackrobes* (Black River Falls, Wisconsin: Ho-Chunk Heritage Preservation Department, undated).

[16] Randy Tallmadge, Hocak Wazijaci Language and Culture Program, author's interview in Mauston, Wisconsin, November 18, 1997.

[17] *Since 1634: In the Wake of Nicolet* is an excellent documentary chronicling the histories of the Menominee and Ho-Chunk people from Nicolet's arrival to the early 1990s, produced

by Dave Erickson and co-produced by Lance Tallmadge, Ho-Chunk, and Alan Caldwell, Menominee (Spring Green, Wisconsin: Ootek Productions, 1993).

[18] *Ibid.*

[19] The Ho-Chunk newspapers have chronicled the tribal bison herd. For more, see: "Where the Buffalo Roam," *Ho-Chunk Wo-Lduk,* Vol. x, No. 21, July 15, 1996, 4; "HCN Farm Hosts Bison and Effigy Mounds Mini-tours," *Hocak Worak,* Vol. xii, No. 16, July 29, 1998, 1; and "Bison Project Gets Shot in the Hide," *Hocak Worak,* Vol. xiii, No. 20, December 20, 1999.

[20] The Ho-Chunk tribal newspaper has documented the tribe's struggle to acquire a portion of the decommissioned site. See "Ho-Chunk Nation Considers Badger Plant," *Hocak Worak,* Vol. xii, No. 7, March 31, 1998, 1; "HCN Receives Support in Badger Land Plan," *Hocak Worak,* Vol. xii, No. 23, Nov. 25, 1998, 1; and "Ho-Chunk Blocked from Local RAB," *Hocak Worak,* Vol. xiii, No. 9, May 10, 1999, 1.

Chapter 5 Notes

[1] Edward Benton-Banai, an Ojibwe medicine man, recounts the Ojibwe migration story in chapter fourteen of *The Mishomis Book,* a spiritual history of the Ojibwe people originally published in 1988 by Red School House in St. Paul, Minnesota. The book was written at the request of parents and educators in the Twin Cities area who recognized the need for culture-based educational materials. Still in print, *The Mishomis Book* is distributed by Indian Country Communications in Hayward, Wisconsin.

[2] Josephine Denomie, a student at St. Mary's School in Odanah, discussed Tagwagane in her essay, "History of Our Nation," included in *Noble Lives of a Noble Race* (Minneapolis: The Brooks Press, 1908).

[3] From 1936 to 1942, Sister Macaria Murphy of St. Mary's School in Odanah interviewed elders about traditional activities, such as ricing and sugaring, as part of a Works Progress Administration (WPA) historical project. The compilation is available on microfilm in the Wisconsin Historical Society Archives, WIHV91-A679, reel 532. Another excellent source on Ojibwe ricing is Thomas Vennum, Jr.'s, *Wild Rice and the Ojibway People* (St. Paul: Minnesota Historical Society Press, 1988).

[4] Lone Man's comments were included in the minutes to the 1825 treaty at Prairie du Chien. See *Documents Relating to the Negotiation of Ratified and Unratified Treaties with Various Tribes of Indians, 1801–1869* (Record Group 75, records of the Bureau of Indian Affairs). Ron Satz provides the major Ojibwe treaties and minutes to the treaties as appendices in "Chippewa Treaty Rights," Transactions of the Wisconsin Academy of Sciences, Arts and Letters (Vol. 79, No. 1). *Ojibway Oratory,* compiled by Mark Diedrich, is a fine collection of speeches delivered by Ojibwe chiefs and headmen between 1695 and 1889 (Rochester, Minnesota: Coyote Books, 1990).

[5] David Wrone, *Economic Impact of the 1837 and 1842 Chippewa Treaties* (Stevens Point, Wisconsin: D. R. Wrone, 1989).

[6] The Ojibwe's understanding of the 1837, 1842, and 1854 treaties was detailed in the 1864 document "Statement Made by the Indians: A Bilingual Petition," which was published in

1988 by the University of Western Ontario as part of its series Studies in the Interpretation of Canadian Native American Languages and Cultures. The document is in the Wisconsin Historical Society Archives, Madison.

7 Benjamin Armstrong provided a fascinating account of the events leading up to and concluding with the 1854 treaty, including the Sandy Lake debacle, in *Early Life among the Indians* (Ashland, Wisconsin: Press of A. W. Bowron, 1892).

8 Martin's evaluation of her Ojibwe servant is contained in a 1903 letter to Samuel Campbell, who served as Indian Agent at La Pointe from 1899 until 1913. See Mrs. J. Martin to Campbell, December 12, 1903, in the Samuel Campbell Papers, Wisconsin Historical Society Manuscript Collections, River Falls Area Research Center, River Falls, Wisconsin. Campbell's papers formed the basis for chapters on Ojibwe allotment and boarding schools in Patricia Loew, "Newspapers and the Lake Superior Chippewa in the 'unProgressive' Era" (doctoral dissertation, University of Wisconsin–Madison, 1998).

9 This account of the Lac Courte Oreilles was compiled from oral history the author collected in 1997–1998 for Celebrating Wisconsin's Native American Heritage, a public history project coordinated by the Great Lakes Intertribal Council as part of the Wisconsin Sesquicentennial commemoration. Source material also came from interviews I conducted with tribal members James Schlender, Jerry Smith, and others for *The Center of the Earth: The Chippewa Flowage after 75 Years,* an educational video produced in 1999 by the Institute for Environmental Studies, University of Wisconsin–Madison. Additional historical background came from *Where the River is Wide: Pahquahwong and the Chippewa Flowage,* by Charlie Otto Rasmussen (Odanah, Wisconsin: Great Lakes Indian Fish & Wildlife Commission Press, 1998).

10 Dozens of tribal members, including Headflyer, testified before a U.S. Senate Subcommittee that traveled to Wisconsin to take testimony during fall 1909. These accounts were published a year later in Condition of Indian Affairs in Wisconsin (Washington, D.C.: Government Printing Office, 1910). Headflyer's testimony may be found on pp. 713–715 and 751–753.

11 This account of the Lac du Flambeau derives from the author's interviews with tribal elders, including Joe Chosa, George Brown, Sr., and Tinker Schuman in 1997–1998 for the Celebrating Wisconsin's Native American Heritage project; from the Samuel Campbell Papers; Albert Cobe's recollections of the Lac du Flambeau Boarding School in the autobiographical *Great Spirit* (Chicago: Childrens Press, 1970); and *Reflections of the Lac du Flambeau,* an illustrated history of Lac du Flambeau, Wisconsin, 1745–1995, compiled by Ben Guthrie, written and edited by Michael J. Goc (Friendship, Wisconsin: New Past Press, 1995).

12 The Red Cliff account is based on the author's interviews with Red Cliff tribal members Leo LeFrenier and Joe Bresette in September 1997 and Walt Bresette in May 1998 as part of the Celebrating Wisconsin's Native American Heritage project. Additional material came from the Campbell Papers; from *Condition of Indian Affairs in Wisconsin;* and from Edmund Danziger's *The Chippewas of Lake Superior* (Norman, Oklahoma: University of Oklahoma Press, 1990).

13 The oral history in this section came from interviews with Dana Jackson, Bad River tribal historian, in August 1997 and September 1999, and with Joe Rose, Bad River elder and

Director of American Indian Studies at Northland College, in August 1997. Information about St. Mary's School was drawn from the *Journal of Sister M. Cunigunda Urbany* compiled by Sister Bonaventure Schoeberle, 1883, Franciscan Sisters of Perpetual Adoration Archives, La Crosse, Wisconsin; letters from tribal members to the Bureau of Catholic Indian Missions, 1897–1915; the Samuel Campbell Papers; and *The Condition of Indian Affairs in Wisconsin*. For more detailed citations, see Patricia Loew, "Natives, Newspapers, and 'Fighting Bob': Wisconsin Chippewa in the 'unProgressive' Era," in *Journalism History*, Vol. 23, Number 4 (Winter 1997–98), and the author's dissertation, "Newspapers and the Lake Superior Chippewa in the 'unProgressive Era.'"

14 Oral history accounts for the Sokaogon section draw heavily from interviews with the hereditary chief of the Sokaogon, Charles Ackley, along with tribal members Fred Ackley and Fran VanZile, in Mole Lake, October 18–20, 1999. Additional material came from Satz's *Chippewa Treaty Rights*.

15 Very little written information exists about the St. Croix Ojibwe, and much of the oral history is speculative. Most of the information I was able to collect on the St. Croix came from interviews with tribal historian Gene Connor in Hertel, Wisconsin, in September 1997 and in a telephone interview on September 29, 1999.

16 Alison Bernstein, *American Indians and World War II* (Norman, Oklahoma: University of Oklahoma Press, 1991), 46.

17 Between 1992 and 1994, Wisconsin Historical Society researchers interviewed 115 Wisconsin women, including several Ojibwe, about their experiences during World War II. Some of the material in this section draws from these interviews, along with my article "Back of the Homefront: Oral Histories of Native American and African-American Wisconsin Women During World War II," *Wisconsin Magazine of History*, Vol. 82, No. 2 (Winter 1998–99). Alison Bernstein provides a good general history of Native Americans during the wartime period in *American Indians and World War II* (Norman, Oklahoma: University of Oklahoma Press, 1991).

18 Much of the material on the Chippewa Treaty Rights disputes is distilled from interviews the author collected while covering the boat landing demonstrations during 1988–1994 as a news reporter for WKOW-TV (ABC) and WHA-TV (PBS). Also, see Patty Loew, "Hidden Transcripts in the Chippewa Treaty Rights Dispute: a Twice-Told Story," *American Indian Quarterly*, Vol. 22, No. 1 (Winter 1998) and *Spring of Discontent* (WKOW-TV documentary produced by Patty Loew), which aired statewide on ABC affiliates in Wisconsin in May 1990. Two excellent resources on the topic are *Chippewa Treaty Rights* by Ron Satz and *Walleye Warriors* by Rick Whaley and Walt Bresette (Philadelphia: New Society Publishers, 1994).

19 For the Ojibwe, Seventh Generation Philosophy is a fundamental belief dictating that present plans must be weighed upon their perceived impact on future generations. This ontology places value on sustainable resource management and long-range planning.

Chapter 6 Notes

1 The Ojibwe and Odawa refer to the three tribes as the Anishinabe or Anishinabeg Alliance. Much of the oral history included in this chapter came from Jim Thunder, a

Potawatomi elder and former tribal chair, who guest-lectured in the author's American Indian Studies seminar on Wisconsin Indians (AIS 450), University of Wisconsin–Madison, on March 2, 1998.

2 In 1988, Shup-Shewana (Howard Lahurreau), an elder of the Keewatinosagiganing Potawatomi Nation (Canada), wrote a fascinating historical account of the Potawatomi than spans more than 30,000 years. Shup-Shewana translated songs and scrolls of the Midewiwin, the Ne shna bek traditional religion, and described the medicinal usages of native plants by the Potawatomi. According to Shup-Shewana, "The Confederacy of the Three Fires Ojibwa-Odawa-Pottawatomie took place in or about 31899 [1,200 years BP, or 796 AD] at Michilimackinac, and was a loose unit of many bands of related people. As time went forward this group of bands became more distant, and generally came together to fight off the thrusts of the Sioux and Iroquois." This little-known manuscript, written in Potawatomi with an English translation, also explained the clan structure and cultural activities of the tribe. *Potawatomi Nation in Canada* (Mactier, Ontario: Keewatinosagiganing Potawatomi Nation Cultural Council, 33103 [1988]), 120.

3 Clarice Ritchie, Potawatomi elder and historian, author's interview in Crandon, Wisconsin, April 4, 2000.

4 R. David Edmunds has several excellent chapters on the Potawatomi role in the French fur trade in *The Potawatomis: Keepers of the Fire* (Norman, Oklahoma: University of Oklahoma Press, 1978).

5 Lyman Copeland Draper, who intended to write a biography of Tecumseh, collected an impressive amount of material on the Shawnee leader, including notes, clippings, and letters about Tecumseh's visits to the Potawatomi and other Indian nations in Wisconsin. This material is part of the Draper Manuscripts, Tecumseh Papers 1811–1931, Wisconsin Historical Society Archives, Madison, Wisconsin. Another good general source on Wis- consin's early history and the activities of the Potawatomi is Alice E. Smith's *The History of Wisconsin, Volume I: From Exploration to Statehood* (Madison: State Historical Society of Wisconsin, 1973).

6 Edmunds, *The Potawatomis*, 220.

7 James Clifton, *The Potawatomi* (New York: Chelsea Publishers, 1987).

8 In 1998, Wisconsin Public Television co-produced an excellent documentary, *The Rush for Grey Gold: How Wisconsin Began,* which described the impact of lead mining on the Indian nations of southwestern Wisconsin and the resulting land loss (Madison, Wisconsin: Ootek Productions and Wisconsin Public Television, 1998).

9 Information about the treaty period came largely from *Potawatomi Tribe,* a historical pamphlet written by Jim Thunder (Cottage Grove, Wisconsin: Jim Thunder, 1993), and "Keeper of the Fire: Potawatomi Tribal History" from *Forest County Potawatomi Nation: Keeper of the Fire* (Crandon, Wisconsin: Forest County Potawatomi Nation, undated). Additional oral history and written materials came from Clarice Ritchie, Jim Thunder, and Billy Daniels during discussions for a public history exhibit sponsored by the tribes to commemorate the Wisconsin Sesquicentennial in May 1998.

10 Recounted by Jim Thunder, tribal historian and former tribal chair of the Forest County Potawatomi.

11 George T. Amour, "My Birthplace: The McCord Indian Village," unpublished memoirs in the possession of Robert Birmingham, State Archaeologist of Wisconsin, April 20, 1992, 1. Big Drum or Dream Dancing, as it is sometimes described, was a pan-Indian religion introduced to the Ne shna bek by the Sioux. According to oral tradition, a young Santee Sioux woman who survived the slaughter of her village by the U.S. cavalry had a vision that directed her to carry a drum to other Indian nations in a spirit of peace and friendship. The Ne shna bek, traditional enemies of the Sioux, received the first drum sometime in the late 1870s. Today, many Potawatomi continue their memberships in Big Drum societies and the Midewiwin, even as they identify themselves as members of Christian religions.

12 In September 1909, Chief Kish-ki-kaam and other Potawatomi testified before a U.S. Senate panel, which included Senator Robert M. ("Fighting Bob") La Follette of Wisconsin. After taking Ojibwe testimony in Shell Lake, Ashland, Lac Courte Oreilles, and Lac du Flambeau, the senators visited the Potawatomi who were living near Laona. A year after the hearings, the testimony of the Potawatomi was combined with that of other Wisconsin Indians and published as the *Condition of Indian Affairs in Wisconsin* (Washington, D.C: Government Printing Office, 1910). Kish-ki-kaam's testimony is on pp. 793–794.

13 Although there are no detailed postwar histories of the Indian nations in Wisconsin., there are several good general histories which contain chapters on termination and relocation. These include Peter Nabokov, *Native American Testimony* (New York: Viking, 1991); Frederick E. Hoxie, *Indians in American History* (Chicago: The Newberry Library, 1988); and Peter Iverson, *We Are Still Here* (Wheeling, Illinois: Harlan Davidson, Inc.).

14 *The Potawatomi Traveling Times* is a twice-monthly publication and one of the few Native American newspapers available on-line: http://www.fcpotawatomi.com/Pages/PTT_Home_Page.html.

15 "Potawatomi Share Revenue," *Ojibwe Akiing,* December 1999, 1–2. *Ojibwe Akiing* (Ojibwe Turf) is an independent monthly newspaper published on the Lac Courte Oreilles Reservation devoted to covering issues of interest to the Ojibwe in the Great Lakes Region.

Chapter 7 Notes

1 In deference to the Oneida who are uncomfortable with the term *Iroquois,* I have elected to use the terms *Haudenosaunee, Five Nations,* or *Six Nations* to describe the Confederacy. Oneida scholars, including Carol Cornelius, author of *Iroquois Corn in a Culture-based Curriculum* (Albany: State University of New York Press, 1999), acknowledge the difficulty in avoiding the use of the word *Iroquois,* since its usage has become so widespread. During an interview, she said she preferred to use *On'yote:aka* or *Oneida* when referring to her nation or the terms *Five Nations* or *Six Nations* when referring to the Confederacy. Carol Cornelius interview, Oneida, Wisconsin, March 9, 2000.

2 The story of Hiawatha and the Great Law of Peace is well known to generations of Haudenosaunee. One of the most popular versions is contained in *American Indian Myths and*

Legends, edited by Richard Erdoes and Alfonso Ortiz (New York: Pantheon Books, 1984), 193–199.

3 William A. Starna, "The Oneida Homeland in the Seventeenth Century" in Jack Campisi and Laurence M. Hauptman, *The Oneida Indian Experience* (Syracuse: Syracuse University Press, 1988), 19. *The Oneida Indian Experience* offers perspectives from contemporary scholars, including linguists, anthropologists, and historians as well as oral history accounts from Oneida elders and community leaders. Along with *The Oneida Indian Journey* edited by Laurence Hauptman and L. Gordon McLester III (Madison: University of Wisconsin Press, 1999), it is an excellent resource on the Wisconsin Oneida.

4 Starna, "The Oneida Homeland in the Seventeenth Century," 13.

5 Author's interview with Loretta Metoxen, Oneida Tribal Historian, Oneida, Wisconsin, March 9, 2000.

6 The original source for the many good general and regional histories about the French fur trade era is Reuben Gold Thwaites's multivolume *Jesuit Relations* (1925). Thwaites used mission accounts compiled by the Jesuit missionaries in North America from 1610 to 1791. The Wisconsin Historical Society has archived additional material collected but not used by Thwaites. See Jesuit Relations Papers, Wisconsin Historical Society Manuscripts Collection, Madison, Wisconsin.

7 For more about the Oneida role in the American Revolution, see Barbara Graymont, "The Oneidas and the American Revolution," in Campisi and Hauptman, *The Oneida Indian Experience,* 31–42.

8 Loretta Metoxen, "Oneida Traditions," *Ibid.,* 145–146. The Oneida Nation of New York (a community separate but culturally related to the Oneida of Wisconsin) has a link from its official Web site devoted to Cooper that includes oral history written down by the nineteenth-century chief William Honyost Rockwell, as well as sketches and a seven-minute video: http://oneida-nation.net/polly-cooper.html.

9 Hauptman and McLester, *The Oneida Indian Journey,* 23.

10 Interview with Cornelius. For more information about this period in Oneida history, see Carol Cornelius, "Examining the Forces After the American Revolution Which Impacted our Move to Wisconsin," and Judy Cornelius, "Eleazer Williams and Albert G. Ellis." Both papers were delivered to the Oneida History Conference, Oneida, Wisconsin, October 23, 1998; copies in author's possession. The Oneida land loss and resulting migration is covered extensively in Hauptman and McLester, *The Oneida Indian Journey.*

11 Loretta Metoxen, "Subdivide and Conquer: The Dawes Allotment Act," *Oneida Cultural Heritage Department Newsletter,* No. 6 (undated).

12 Like most Indian nations reorganized under the 1934 Act, the Oneida adopted a constitution that delineated legislative, executive, and judiciary branches within its "General Tribal Council." The Oneida constitution, which was revised in August 1998, continues to adhere to this trifurcated form of government.

13 Unnamed Oneida elder, quoted in Rosalie M. Robertson's "Oneida Educational Planning" in Campisi and Hauptman, *The Oneida Indian Experience,* 166. In September 1997, I

spoke to several Oneida elders during a visit to gather research for a public history exhibit commemorating the State of Wisconsin Sesquicentennial. One woman, who wished to remain anonymous, told me that while she made "some friends I stayed close to all my life . . . that first Christmas was really hard. I cried the whole day, I was so homesick."

14 Military records and oral history indicate that the Oneida participated in and supported the efforts in both world wars; however, no detailed history has yet been written. Two excellent general histories of Native Americans during the war years are *American Indians in World War I,* by Thomas A. Britten (Albuquerque, New Mexico: University of New Mexico Press, 1997), and *American Indians and World War II,* by Alison R. Bernstein (Norman, Oklahoma: University of Oklahoma Press, 1991).

15 Information about contemporary Oneida activities came from the tribe's promotional brochure; from "Development and Enterprises" in *Oneida Nation* (Oneida, Wisconsin: Oneida Nation, undated); and from the author's interviews with Carol Cornelius, Loretta Metoxen, Kirby Metoxen, and Keith Skenandore in September 1997 and May 2000.

16 The Wisconsin Oneida have asserted their claims not only through the courts but also through a vigorous community relations campaign. For additional background information, see "Land Claims Settlement or Land Rights Sell-Out?" (p. 21) and "Chronology of the Oneida Land Claims" (p. 23) in *Kalihwesaks,* Vol. 305 (December 31, 1998); and "Land Claim Issue Not New for Judge" (p. 22), "Summaries of Indian Land Claims" (p. 22), and "New York Development Directed to Discontinue Activities" (p. 23) in *Kalihwesaks,* Vol. 313 (April 8, 1999).

Chapter 8 Notes

1 Mohican Nation, Stockbridge-Munsee Band, *Brief History of the Mohican Nation, Stockbridge-Munsee Band* (Bowler, Wisconsin: Stockbridge-Munsee Historical Committee, 1996), 3.

2 In her history of the Mohicans (1852), Electa Jones described the Wi-gow-wauw, or chief sachem, as a leader, "chosen by the nation, whom they looked upon as conductor and promoter of their general welfare." The office was hereditary "by the lineage of a female's offspring, but not on the man's line, but on woman's part." When he died, a nephew (a son of his sister) was appointed to the office, "not any of his sons." *Stockbridge, Past and Present* (Springfield, Massachusetts: Samuel Bowles & Company, 1854), 20.

3 *Ibid.*, 22.

4 This account, attributed to Hendrick Aupaumut at an Indian conference in 1754, is quoted in both Patrick Frazier, *The Mohicans of Stockbridge* (Lincoln, Nebraska: University of Nebraska Press, 1992), 2–3, and Shirley Dunn, *The Mohicans and Their Land, 1609–1730* (Fleischmanns, New York: Purple Mountain Press, 1994), 18.

5 Relations between the Mohawks and the Mohicans warmed after a Mohican chief married a Mohawk woman. Their son, Hendrick, became one of the most celebrated Mohawk leaders. In 1710, Hendrick and the Mohican sachem Etowaukaum traveled to England together to meet with Queen Anne. Frazier, Mohicans of Stockbridge, 9.

6 *Ibid.,* 13.

7 Author's interview with the Mohican Nation, Stockbridge-Munsee Band Historical Committee, including Dorothy Davids, Sheila Powless, Bernice Miller Pigeon, and Ruth Gudinas in Bowler, Wisconsin, October 1997.

8 In a 1782 letter to the New York General Assembly, Johannis Mtohksin, Jacob Nanauphtaunk, Solomon Uhhaunauwaunmut, and the "sons of King Ben" asked that some of their ancestral land along the Hudson River and Lake Champlain be returned to them. "Brother," they wrote, "what I ask is that you resign to me that land, which is justly mine, which I have neither sold or given to you; or give me its value, that I may get food and cloathing for myself, my women and children and be happy with you as formerly." Quoted in Frazier, *Mohicans of Stockbridge,* 235.

9 There is woefully little secondary material on the Brothertown (also referred to as the Brotherton) Indians. My sources include the pamphlet *The Brothertown Indian Nation of Wisconsin Brief History* (Beaver Dam, Wisconsin: Brothertown History Committee, 1982), by Jack Campisi, and interviews with June Ezold, Brothertown Tribal Chair, in Arbor Vitae, Wisconsin, September 1997, and by telephone during the spring of 1998.

10 *Brief History of the Mohican Nation, Stockbridge-Munsee Band,* 6.

11 *Ibid.*

12 Annie Paprocki, "On New Ground: The Life of Electa Quinney" (unpublished paper, 1999, in author's possession), and "Electa Quinney: Kaukauna and the State's First Female Schoolteacher," *Kaukauna Times,* April 7, 1994.

13 Campisi, *The Brothertown Indian Nation of Wisconsin.*

14 Ezold, phone interview, July 2000.

15 *Youth of the Mohican Nation, Stories of Our Elders* (Gresham, Wisconsin: Muh-he-con-neew Press, 1999), 10.

16 Davids, phone interview, June 2000.

17 Pigeon, phone interview, June 2000.

18 Davids, phone interview, June 2000.

19 *Ibid.*

20 *Ibid.*

21 Pigeon, phone interview, June 2000.

22 Ezold, phone interview, July 2000.

Resources and Further Reading

Books and Journals

Benton-Banai, Edward. *The Mishomis Book.* St. Paul: Red School House, 1988 (distributed by Indian Country Communications, Hayward, Wisconsin).

Robert Bieder. *Native American Communities in Wisconsin, 1600–1960.* Madison: University of Wisconsin Press, 1995.

Campisi, Jack and Hauptman, Laurence M. *The Oneida Indian Experience.* New York: Syracuse University Press, 1988.

Edmunds, R. David. *The Potawatomis: Keepers of the Fire.* Norman, Oklahoma: University of Oklahoma Press, 1978.

Frazier, Patrick. *The Mohicans of Stockbridge.* Lincoln, Nebraska: University of Nebraska Press, 1992.

Hauptman, Laurence M. and McLester, L. Gordon. *The Oneida Indian Journey.* Madison: University of Wisconsin Press, 1999.

Jones, Electa F. *Stockbridge, Past and Present.* Salem, Massachusetts: Higginson Book Co., 1854.

Lurie, Nancy Oestrich, *Mountain Wolf Woman.* Ann Arbor, Michigan: University of Michigan Press, 1961.

Ourada, Patricia, *The Menominee Indians: A History.* Norman, Oklahoma: University of Oklahoma Press, 1979.

Satz, Ron. "Chippewa Treaty Rights." *Transactions,* Vol. 79, No. 1, Wisconsin Academy of Sciences, Arts and Letters.

Shames, Deborah. *Freedom with Reservation: The Menominee Struggle to Save Their Land and People.* Washington, D.C.: National Committee to Save the Menominee People and Forests, 1972.

Tanner, Helen Hornbeck. *Atlas of Great Lakes Indian History.* Norman, Oklahoma: Published for the Newberry Library by the University of Oklahoma Press, 1987.

Whaley, Rick and Bresette, Walter. *Walleye Warriors.* Philadelphia: New Society Publishers, 1994.

Videotapes

No Word for Goodbye. Writer/producer, Patty Loew. Madison: WKOW-TV, 1986.

The Rush for Grey Gold. Writer/producer, Dave Erickson. Spring Green, Wisconsin: Ootek Productions, 1998.

Since 1634: In the Wake of Nicolet. Writer/producer, Dave Erickson; Ho-Chunk co-producer, Lance Tallmadge; Menominee co-producer, Alan Caldwell. Spring Green, Wisconsin: Ootek Productions, 1993.

The Spring of Discontent. Writer/producer, Patty Loew. Madison: WKOW-TV, 1990.

Thunder in the Dells. Producers, Dave Erickson and Lance Tallmadge. Spring Green, Wisconsin: Ootek Productions, 1992.

CD-ROMs/Web Sites

Brothertown Indians: http://www-unix.oit.umass.edu/~astephen/bro.html

College of the Menominee Nation: http://www.menominee.edu

Forest County Potawatomi: http://www.fcpotawatomi.com

Great Lakes Indian Fish and Wildlife Commission (with links to each Ojibwe Band in Wisconsin and member bands in Michigan and Minnesota): http://glifwc.org

Great Lakes Inter-Tribal Council (with links to each Indian Nation in Wisconsin): http://www.glitc.org

Ho-Chunk Nation: http://www.ho-chunk.com

Lac Courte Oreilles Community College: http://www.lco-college.edu

Lac Courte Oreilles Tribal School: http://www.lcoschools.org

Lac du Flambeau Public School: http://www.ldf.k12.wi.us

Maawanji'ding: Gathering Together (CD-ROM). Brain-Box Digital Archives (Collinsville, Connecticut: hup!multimedia, inc., 1998).

Menominee Nation Web site: http://www.menominee.nsn.us

Mohican Nation, Stockbridge-Munsee Band Web site: http://www.mohican.com

Oneida Nation Web site: http://www.oneidanation.org

Oneida History (CD-ROM). Bear Claw Research (Oneida: Bear Claw Research, 1998).

Wisconsin Tribal Communities (Web site maintained by Milwaukee Public Museum with links to each of the Indian Nations): http://192.206.48.3/wirp/ICW-05.html

Index